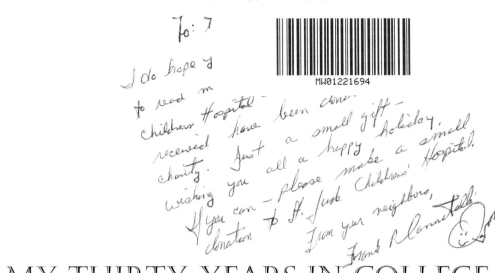

To: 7

I do hope y
to read m
childrens Hospital - have been come-
received Just a small gift -
charity. all a happy holiday.
wishing you please make a small
If you can to St. Jude Childrens' Hospital.
donation From your neighbors,
Frank Cannatelli

MY THIRTY YEARS IN COLLEGE

A Retired Teachers Memories of University Life at Southern
Connecticut State University: A Tribute to Students, Professors, and Administrators

Best Wishes!

Frank P. Cannatelli, Esquire

Cover Photo by Laramie Marchant-Shapiro

TABLE OF CONTENTS

DEDICATION

This book is dedicated first to the many thousands of students I met and had the privilege of teaching over the years. Most of my students have become successful and productive members of society; all of my students have made me very proud to be apart of their learning and of their lives. Every student has touched me significantly. For that, I give my sincere thanks.

Second, I also dedicate this book to my wonderful colleagues at Southern. I recognize all of our wonderful secretaries through the years, including Jean, Noreen and Monica, and also our wonderful maintenance staff. This is done to simply acknowledge how vital these people are to the mission of the school. Without them, the place would be truly in a state of suspended animation. We all would be bright but bewildered, and the hallways filled with muck, candy wrappers, empty milk cartons, and you get my drift.

One of my fondest recollections is that of a maintenance man named Mack, who maintained Seabury Hall, the building which originally housed our Political Science Department. Mack would always be in promptly at 6 a.m. and would often tell me that he had to get in early so Jean would not come looking for him. He really did not want any problems with Jean. Well, with all candor, most of us in the Department were also afraid of getting on Jean's "bad side". The first golden rule of thumb was to never, and I mean never, cross Jean. Jean was the heart of our Department. She was always a hard-working no-nonsense person; Jean kept us all in line. She kept the Department sailing calmly. No one ever could pull the wool over her eyes because

Jean simply was too sharp to let that happen. Some of us who were brave enough to try, simply learned the hard way. Jean could not be fooled, just take it from me when I tell you that. She knew about those tricky efforts before anyone could even try them. Jean, was like our current Secretary Monica; She (like Monica) is the very best. She symbolizes the hard work and the dedication which personifies all of us. These women were more than mere secretaries. They were/are our confidants, our egos or alter egos, our memories, our friends, our symbolic mothers, our sisters, and simply the part of us that makes "our department" a family. Like a true family, the department is similar pure and simple due to the wonderful work of our secretaries throughout the years. This function is often overlooked but cherished. It signifies a great department. It really does.

In any event, our Department owes a great debt of gratitude to these fine women. Their difficult efforts day in and day out make our jobs so much easier. God Bless these great women who never get the credit they deserve. They are and will always be great role models. To put it in a nutshell, beside any great professor/teacher is most definitely a great secretary. The place simply does not function well without these people. They are so little praised but so vital. Thank you so very much for being there.

Third and last, but surely not least, I cannot forget my wonderful colleagues: Dr. Kul B. Rai, Dr. Paul J. Best, Dr. David F. Walsh, Dr. Arthur Paulson, Dr. Harriet B. Applewhite, Dr. John O. Iatrides, Dr. John Critzer, and the late Dr. Pamela Rendiro, all

Professors Emeritus. These were and are excellent people who always tried to make the Department and the University better. Their efforts cannot be forgotten since all have paved the way for the current staff today. They were/are the ground-setters or the foundation. With such a solid rock, the newer professors have the benefit of the old. The chain goes back linking all of us together in this way. Tradition means a lot to us.

Dr. Rai is a soft-spoken man, who taught us the virtues of his wisdom and kindness. He would often remind me and the others how fortunate we are to be teachers at Southern, and how we are there to serve our students. Whenever I would get upset with a student and want to act rashly, I would always remember Dr. Rai's words. I learned to take a deep breath, and to never act without first thinking and weighing all options. I would consider and reconsider my position, and when in doubt, discuss my options with my dear colleagues. After much thought and deliberation, I would then act carefully and always try to act in the best interests of the student and the School. Sometimes I would have to weigh the equities and then proceed with caution. It was never an easy task. I thank Dr. Rai for his many years of service and inspiration. He showed me creativity in dealing with students. Good professors are often unique in the way they do things. I call it the Midas Touch. How we deal with things is indicative of who we are. Kul had the Midas touch. His uniqueness made us all unique. It was almost similar to osmosis. He had it and when we got close to him, it simply rubbed-off on us and we absorbed it. Knowing and working with Kul was magic. The spell was real. He made the education experience at Southern a wonderful and beautiful thing for staff and students. He is truly missed.

Dr. Best, a big and tall man, would often come across as a tough guy, but in reality simply is a "nice guy". There were times I upset him only to realize that he is a great person. The truth of the matter, or truth be told, that Paul simply is the type of guy who does not want anyone to know he is a great guy. I take solace in the fact that although he generally does not like lawyers, that maybe-just-maybe, I am the exception. Paul taught most of us not to be too soft when dealing with our students. He did not want me or anyone else to give the school away to the students. Unlike Doctor Rai, Paul was strict, but only demanded that students work hard to succeed. He always had the best interests of the students in mind. If there were extremes in the Department, Dr. Rai would be on one side and Dr. Best would be on the other side. Understand though, that I am not trying to criticize either one's approach. This dichotomy of Rai/Best or Best/Rai almost sounds like an advertisement for the best type of sandwich to order at the deli. I guess if it is a sandwich, Rai-Best (Rye) is the better order of things. I suppose you could order "Best" on "Rye" if you like. This dichotomy of sorts gave balance to our Department and I cannot emphasize enough the contributions of each man to our Department and University. I do hope I have not disclosed Paul's secret, though, which is safe with all of us. He is a great guy, and well, please don't tell anyone. We should all try to keep Paul's secret. So, please don't tell anyone I spilled the beans.

I probably know Dr. David Walsh the best, with no pun on Paul's name. David and I go back to our UConn days in the seventies. I recall writing my undergraduate "Honors Thesis" while David was writing his "Graduate Thesis". We were writing with Dr. Louis Gerson who happened to be the Political Science Department Chair in those days. David and I would run into each other somewhat frequently at Lou's office prior to meeting

6

with Lou Gerson. Florence was the secretary. She was another nice woman who quite frankly kept her composure when I would have thought her to be high-strung with the number of students pestering her day in and out. (I was one of those students and am Guilty as Charged and Duly Confess.)

As luck would have it, Lou would take me first and David second. Boy, if I were David, I surely would have been upset at that. Thinking back, making Dave wait really did not seem fair. In any event, I took pleasure in making the graduate student wait. I don't know why, but that was/is my personality in a nutshell. David was the better person. He would smile and never complain. He was always a gentleman in that regard. In fact, no matter what the situation would entail, David was simply that type of guy. He was/is always a gentleman. I think that bothered me the most. If the tides were turned, I think I would have surely said something to David. "Hey, you, I got him first or else", or something along those lines. Of course, there is not a mean bone in David's body. He never was mean, and it is not in his nature to be mean. He is, and always will be, a gentleman's gentleman-pure and simple. When I think of David, I think of David and Goliath. Only, David is the gentle giant. He sways people by his huge person-ality. He is a gentle giant with an immense persona and with a great sense of humor.

When I was hired at Southern, and saw David again almost fifteen years later, he recognized me right away. David was quite a character at Southern and always made us laugh. He is a gem of a guy. In fact, I can remember arguing with another professor about student attendance. I mentioned how I really wanted my students to attend class because I wanted my students to participate. The other guy, who I really should not mention, asked me, "why should it matter, are you incompetent or something"? Well, I got up to approach the other guy, and Dr. Rai came in between us. I was hot to say the least. Well, things eventually cooled down, and David came in and said to me, "Frank, I am with you". "I agree one hundred percent with you". The vote of confidence made me feel better, but I was still embarrassed for losing my temper. I am so glad things did not get out of hand that day. It was Kul B. Rai to the rescue. Most people may not appreciate that comment, but if you know Kul you would truly understand. Kul hasn't a violent bone in his body. He broke it up despite that fact.

David informed us about the major union issues and legislative agenda. He was instrumental in making and keeping our Department well-rounded, competitive, and well-respected throughout the University community. His unique and comprehensive understanding of Connecticut politics made our Department thrive. I often compared David's efforts to those of Dr. Gerson's, in that he tried to run our Department much like Lou Gerson ran his Department when we attended UConn. David made the whole ball of wax run well. His more than forty years at Southern are remarkable and praiseworthy. Thank you, David, for all you have done here at Southern and for all you continue to do.

Dr. Paulson was hired after I started at Southern, but was full time while I was simply an adjunct. As an aside, though, I must state that at no time did I ever feel unwanted or inferior by me colleagues, even if I were (in fact) inferior in terms of writing, research, or what have you. I think back to Dr. Lee, the forensic expert who worked for the defense in the O.J. Simpson trial. Dr. Lee, an instructor at the University of New Haven,

8

once told me that when he arrived in California to testify the authorities there made him feel distant and not welcome. I thought that this was interesting primarily because we have a man here, Dr. Lee, who is world-renowned for his work and publications. He is one of the very best in his field, and the criminologists and law enforcement personnel in California shunned him. Can you imagine that? I mention this because that is the furthest thing from the truth regarding my colleagues. They took me in, coached me along, and never shunned me. They all made me feel welcome. This speaks volumes about my Department. This made Southern so enjoyable. It is hard to verbalize it in any other way. I was truly fortunate to be included in this wonderful Department.

Art was funny, witty, intelligent, and just a pleasure to work with. He maintained our Department through serious budgetary woes. Those years took their toll on Art. He constantly fought with the Administration to keep key classes running, and some of those key classes were the very classes I taught. He fought to keep me on, when all other Departments were unable to keep their adjuncts on. Art could maintain his pace primarily because of his lovely wife, Lynn, whose love and support often spilled over to all of us. I cannot stress how important Art's contributions were to our Department. I know he lost many a night's sleep trying to maintain our struggling Department due to the financial constraints placed upon the University. Art never buckled and continued to lead us on. He was our "fearless leader". Art definitely deserves credit for his long hours and dedication to the Department. Thank you, Art, for all you have done. I for some reason don't think you have ever been given the proper credit you deserve. You were a true leader and are sorely missed. We lost the wind behind our sails when you retired. Art had heart. I will always remember him riding his bike to school in the snow. I always wanted to yell at him, "you nut", but we all knew he was our nutty professor. After all, who rides their bike in the snow? Surely not me. Yes, Art would ride his bike in the snow by golly smiling and jolly while he rode. What a guy. He was so much fun and a pleasure to be around. The place was never the same once Art left. He and Lynn made the Department very special. They are so special.

Dr. Harriet Applewhite was an adjunct and later invited to apply for head of our Honors' College. She worked hard to make the honors college what it is today. Thank you Harriet for your many gracious and wonderful years of service. You were always a pleasure to work with here at Southern. Your efforts cannot be overstated. I recall Lynn, Art's wife, and I kidding about the difference between the Yale and Harvard students. We joked, and did so while Harriet was teaching a course in the next room which was the Political Science Conference room. Lynn then bit her lip, stating: "Frank, we gotta be careful or else Harriet will here us". We both laughed, because Harriet's husband was a professor at Yale, and we knew she would not appreciate our joking about the Yale students. (You know, at least the Harvard Students aren't afraid to get their hands dirty, not like the Yale students, etc.). Anyhow, Harriet always had a smile and warm heart for everyone she met and instructed. I last saw her at Art's retirement party. She attended with her husband smiling and gracious as always. She is a delightful person.

Dr. John Iatrides was one of our senior professors when I was hired. I felt like I knew John pretty well because my Professor, Lou Gerson, spoke so highly of him when I was at UConn. John was old school, and that meant that you had better tow the line or else. John's contributions and scholarly works put Southern on the map. He was/is an expert on World War Two Recovery, and I can recall his lectures on the Truman Doctrine and Marshall Plan. He was an articulate speaker, and a wonderful role model. Our Department was and is so proud to have Dr. Iatrides here. He was our Department Head for years and his leadership helped improve our Department. John is such a gentleman, and represents the person we all aspire to be. He is a great professor. As I will discuss later, great professors are never forgotten. They are with us always.

Dr. John Critzer, again, was hired after I started at Southern. John is/was a quiet man, but loved by his students and colleagues. He was articulate, intelligent, and he had a unique way of getting his point across. I often would listen to his lectures outside of his class. He was an inspiration to me. He was soft but clearly spoken, and by no means boring. "BORING", is the most cited criticism of professors by their students on our school evaluations. The students loved the way John would present his class materials. Always a gentleman, John was another example of a great role model for students and teachers alike. We all truly miss him. At his retirement party, I remember telling him, "John, it seems like yesterday when they hired you". John responded, "Frank, that was over twenty years ago". I remember everyone there laughing. Everyone roared. John's smile represented the warm inspiration he had on our Department. What a truly nice man. John's contributions to our Department and School cannot go without being noted and mentioned. He left a very fine mark on us all. He too is sorely missed.

The last Emeritus Professor is the late Pamela Rendiro. When I was hired and introduced to Pam, I remembered her face from my UConn days. I recall studying in the Political Science conference room when she came in and sat down and started speaking with me. She introduced herself as a professor from Southern, stating she was there (at UConn) for a staff meeting. She asked me my name, and what my studies were. When I saw Pam at Southern, I mentioned to her that we had in fact met before. She did not recall. When I told her she was at a staff meeting at UConn, she did perk up and say, "Oh yes, probably". Pam was a very conscientious professor. She was always there for her students and did her best to help all of us. I can remember her smile when I would speak to her. She was a gracious woman. I recall going to her retirement party. We had all chipped in for a chair to surprise her, but it had not yet come in by the party. Dr. Rai suggested the idea of giving her a card with a picture of the rocking chair to show her what we had ordered for her. When we gave Pam the card with the picture, she laughed, thinking it was a joke because of her retiring. (It was a picture of the rocking chair.) Dr. Rai had to explain to her that it was no joke, that we had in fact ordered her a chair as her retirement present from the Department. Anyhow, we all laughed because Pam thought it was a joke, and Kul was as serious as could be that it was not a joke. It was a beautiful memory of a wonderful woman. Pam was a special person. She made Southern a better place by her presence and contribution. She was humble, intelligent, and spunky. God rest her soul. Those who knew her truly miss her. She was one of a kind and we were all blessed to have her at Southern.

I would like to thank, as honorable mention, my current colleagues. They include:

Dr. Kevin Buterbaugh, Dr. Patricia Olney, Dr. Costel Calin, Dr. Jennifer Hopper, Dr. Jonathan Wharton, Dr. Jonathan O'Hara and Dr. Theresa Marchant-Shapiro. Hopefully I did not forget anyone, but if I did, my true apologies as any lapse of memory is mine and mine alone. I take full responsibility for all my shortcomings of this book. With the exception of Professors Buterbaugh, Olney, O'Hara, and Marchant-Shapiro, who have all been with the Department for a long time, I must acknowledge the hard work of the newer professors who are now taking over. They include: Professors Wharton, Calin and Hopper. These people are blessed with keeping the tradition going at Southern. All of their contributions cannot be ignored. Thank you so much for all of your wonderful efforts. Dr. Calin has been instrumental in throwing some of the best parties ever.

Last, I must also mention a few of my professors I had while at the University of Connecticut. I mention these professors simply because of their impact on me and my desire to teach. I think back to the Political Science Department at UConn in the seventies, and realize that I am so lucky to have a similar group of colleagues at Southern. With true love and admiration, I compare these past professors to my excellent colleagues today.

The Professor I enjoyed the most was Dr. Louis Gerson. Dr. Walsh and I recently attended a memorial service for Lou at UConn which brought back so many fond memories. Lou was soft spoken, and kind. He was always industrious, personable, and a great role model. He was a tall man, but gentle in both his appearance and mannerism. It was his love of teaching and education that inspired me to teach.

More will be mentioned of him later. There were other professors that also had an impact on me. I will be mentioning and discussing all of them so briefly truly not doing justice to them or their unique contribution to their students, their University, or their field. Their memories are truly kept alive by their unique contribution to me which I have tried to pass on to my students. They will be discussed later.

I need to further mention my late nephew Domenic, whose memory is with me daily. His death has caused an immense loss on my family. Domenic was such a wonderful person, and was always fun to see and be with. I have come to cherish his little boy, Luca, born shortly after his father's death. It pains me to know that Domenic never had the chance, even once, to hold his little boy. As Luca grows up, I hope that I am able to share those precious moments I had with his father with him. In this way I can try to keep Domenic's memory alive.

In some respects, this is one purpose of my book. The best way to honor someone is to keep their memory alive. We learn from them and keep their contributions alive. We remember and honor them as we live their memory and contribution.

Further, with fond memories, I must mention the late President Michael Adante, whose contribution to Southern cannot be overlooked. Mike worked hard to improve our University. The beautiful buildings and great physical plant that our students now enjoy are all due to Mike's effort to make Southern competitive. As a graduate of Southern, Mike was always proud to lead and improve our University. He is truly missed by all who knew him. He was to date the greatest President of Southern Connecticut State University. This great school, with its many improvements, is a shrine to his memory. We were fortunate to have him as our Civic Leader and our President. We are so proud of him. We are fortunate to have his memories with us to help us endure the rough times. We all strive in our hearts and efforts to contribute to the betterment of our great University and remain motivated by Mike's efforts and memory. He is sorely missed.

Finally, one caveat is in order. My book in many ways is an autobiography because it includes a large part of my life. It actually includes the better part of my life. The book includes my memories of facts and of events. It is therefore written from my memory. I truly apologize if my recollection of facts and events are different from those of other people mentioned in this book. Again, I take full responsibility for any and all errors simply alerting the reader that no error made here was knowingly or intelligently made to harm anyone. Also, I do not intend to invade anyone's privacy rights either.

Dated at Wallingford this 15th day of April of 2018.

Frank P. Cannatelli
Professor of Political Science/
Esquire
Cannatellilaw@aol.com

PREFACE/INTRODUCTION TO BOOK

This is a short book which is actually made up of my memories and stories of events. The stories are true with some funny and others serious. The lessons are often ironic. You would expect that most of the lessons mentioned are about my classes and my students. This is correct. What is truly amazing is the way teaching has transformed my life. This is only part of the story though. The book tries to weave a mosaic. What appears to be incoherent eventually becomes very coherent.

Once at the doctor's office, the nurse asked me if I was ever depressed. I thought a second, and responded: " Gee, I simply don't have time to be depressed". She laughed.

The point is simple. If we as teachers, or students, really keep ourselves busy, there is little time left for idle play. With a busy law practice, and a busy teaching schedule, I learned that time is a precious commodity. Time management is key. This applies to students, teachers, and administrators. A minute gone is a minute lost forever.

There is always the need to set a good example. If I am unorganized, it is hard to expect organization from anyone else. If I am strict about dates and times, I must also apply these rules to my game. If I give a test on such and such a date and if I expect my class to be there and prepared, I must have the same discipline apply to me when the class expects that I have my grading done in a timely manner. I would always try to get the midterm tests back and graded by the next class after giving the test. Why? The best way to teach someone is by setting a good example. I remember the boy scout motto: "Always be prepared". It applies to every facet of life and it applies here.

I am trying to say that the rules I force my classes to live by must be the same rules that I force myself to live by. If not, fairness goes out the window and I lose the respect from all of my students. This is not a good thing. The way we learn some basic things is the theme of this book. The way we apply those basic things is also a crucial theme. Of course, learning is never a one-way street. What is good for the goose is good for the gander. I believe the stories shared will illustrate my point. My learning truly began when I started my teaching career.

CHAPTER ONE:

"Simple Generalities And Complex Conclusions"

What makes anyone want to become a teacher? I suppose there are several ways

to address that question. Objectively, or generally, people may want to teach because

they do not like the area they studied as applied in the real world, and feel they can

better contribute by teaching. This approach often leads to a focus on theory.

Subjectively, I think the answer is the opposite. By being a practicing attorney,

I really felt and believed (and still do believe), that by practicing the profession

of law, I could better help students seeking careers in law by bringing my real world

experience into the classroom. I felt I may have an edge over my colleagues in that

regard. Keep in mind that a feeling is not a proven theory. I could be right, and

obviously, I could be wrong. I did hope that I was correct. It was a shot in the dark.

Unfortunately for me when I was hired, some of my colleagues felt that lawyers

having a Juris Doctorate, were simply not as qualified as someone having a PH. D. I

guess I had to figure it out myself. How did I do that? I taught for thirty years always

trying to make the subjects and courses better. Slowly, due to persistence and

nothing else, my colleagues began to realize that I was committed and would go the

extra mile to help my students. President Ford once told me that "time and perseverance

are the keys to success." He was right.

I always understood that teaching like learning is symbiotic. A good teacher must

learn how to improve his/her courses, so he/ she must be a student in that regard. A good student must learn the material such that he/she can master it and apply it to the real world such that he/she often becomes a teacher in that regard. Teaching and Learning are dynamic processes, and never should be static. Thinking back to law school, I can recall my professor coming in, and going through the same book in the same way day in and day out for what seemed to be forever. That example is one of poor teaching. A poor teacher makes it difficult to learn. There was no symbiosis there. I learned that this is clearly not the way to teach a class. I know, some of you are thinking well, he must not have done well in the class. Well, to the contrary, I got an A. My success was not the result of good instruction though. I studied hard and learned what not to do by my professor. So, I suppose I owe him/her thanks in that regard. Sometimes we can succeed even with a bad teacher nonetheless. I never wanted to leave that type of memory with any of my students. If I did I very humbly apologize.

If a student was seeking an internship, but for one reason or another could not find one, I would try to help by offering and/or allowing the student to work in my law office doing some sort of a legal project or working on a real case. If he/she was considering law school and needed advice, I would advise him/her. If he/she needed a letter of reference, I would provide one. If he/she needed a call to a potential employer, like the Attorneys' General Office, or the States' Attorney's Office, I would call. If he/she needed special help, I would try to provide it. If he/she needed someone to travel with him/her to attend a law school forum, I would volunteer. I recall speaking to various law school deans to try to help my students with the law school admission process. I know I annoyed a lot of administrators by my efforts.

If a student was experiencing serious personal issues, I would try to be understanding/accommodating regarding assignments, etc. I truly felt (and still do feel) that it was(is) an honor to be a teacher at Southern, and that I was here to serve my students as best I could. This was the Kul B. Rai motto. I lived by it, keeping in mind the Paul Best admonition not to give the school away. Now, this did not mean I would allow cheating or I would look the other way when a student was attempting to take unfair advantage of other students. I felt that if the student tried, I would try to help any way I could. I would try to meet the student half way. My function was multifaceted. I found that a rigid approach simply did not work well while dealing with undergraduate students. Flexibility of approach was always best. If you were too rigid, it was like trying to place a square peg in a round hole. It did not work.

I simply mean that the rules would be explained early on to my students, and if someone could not abide by the rules for one reason or another, they would be expected to alert me of their issues or problems before they broke the rule(s). Most of my students tried to comply and did mature while taking my classes. They, as well as I, did benefit from each other in the classroom and did learn a lot. This has been truly a rewarding experience that must be noted. Teaching is a humbling experience.

The future chapters include certain times in class, often hilarious and often serious. The sum of the book explains quite clearly why I love to teach. It is the culmination of all the events, learning, and experiences that explain my choice. It was a long journey. It was quite memorable and worth sharing. The simple generalities taught often lead to complex conclusions learned. The symbiosis involved made the process multifaceted and multidimensional for all concerned. The process explained is simply mind blowing and magical.

CHAPTER TWO: Humble Beginnings

IF YOU EVER ARE FORTUNATE ENOUGH TO HAVE A JOB YOU REALLY LOVE, YOU ARE TRULY BLESSED BY GOD.

When I was young, as I think back, I can remember telling my father how much I hated school. Make no bones about it, I hated school. I remember also telling dad that I could not wait to turn sixteen so I could quit. That comment never went over well with my father. Dad was a working man, and never had the opportunity to go beyond the sixth grade. I never understood that because I thought you had to be sixteen to quit. I never inquired why dad only attended school to the sixth grade. He said he had to work to help support his family. I simply left it at that-taking him at his word.

I mention this because despite dad's lack of a formal education, he was quite deceiving. He always read the newspapers, and could converse with anyone about politics, economics and you name it. I can still hear him arguing with family friends, who were all college educated, about stupid reasoning and lack of common sense. I can still hear him arguing "What are you, stupid?", as I would turn red and get embarrassed as he would discuss topics with many friends and relatives. Once dad would make his point the other person would say, "Gee, you're right, I never thought of that". I would then exhale deeply and smile. After all, calling someone stupid surely isn't the best way to "make friends and influence people" if you know what I mean? (Right Dale?). Dad did not care. If you're right, well then, you're right. That was my dad in a nutshell. People who argued with him often bit off more than they could chew. Now I am not saying dad was never wrong. All I am saying is that he was rarely wrong. He was different from my mother. Mom was always right as most moms are.

Despite my father's lack of formal education, I was always proud of the way he could speak up and defend his position better than most people with better education could. Dad was truly amazing in that way. He was self-made and self-taught. You sure as hell could not beat him at checkers or any card games. He was tricky and sneaky and he always would win. Dad was talented. I learned from him that education is more than book learning. A well-rounded person is intelligent in the ways of the world or street smart. Of course, education simply adds to the potion and is the icing on the cake.

When dad would hear me talk about quitting school, he would simply shake his head and say, "well, what will you do with the rest of your life? Did you ever think about that? "Are you interested in a trade, like Pat, (my brother) in carpentry, plumbing", etc., "He would ask me that question because my brother Pat, short for Patrick, was interested in carpentry and in fact became a carpenter. Although his middle name was Patrick, his real name was Joseph Patrick. We never called him Joe. At least, I never did. We all called my brother Pat. I recall one time riding in the truck with him. He slyly stated to me: "You don't even know my whole name". Angrily, I said "IIIIIII know!" Pat smiled when I said, "Joseph Patrick Cannatelli". He said "I didn't think you knew my whole name". I said, "I know it". Pat realized at that moment, that although he thought he knew me well, that in fact, he did not know me as well as he thought. My anger made him realize that I was a bit more observant than he expected.

Now, I digress, but I need to at this point. I forgot to mention that at birth, I was adopted. My family, including my brothers, Jim and Pat, always treated me like their

brother. My parents, including my mother and father, always treated me like their

son. My aunts and uncles, including my Aunt Anne, (my father's sister) always treated

me like their (her) nephew. I say this because when I often would be with my brother

Pat, sometimes-out of the blue-someone would say, "he isn't even your brother" in an

attempt to single me out or embarrass me. The comment, no matter who it came from,

would always hurt me. It would always make me sad. It would always single me out. At

this early age, I learned a little bit about discrimination. I learned what it meant to be

singled out and to be made to feel different. With all that said, my brother Pat would

always, always, always come to my side. He would say "don't you ever say that, Frank is

my kid-brother and don't you ever forget that". I loved him so much for that. He would

always be there for me. He would protect me. He always had a way of doing that. I

mention this because it later meant so much to me when my department accepted me

despite my being different in so many ways from my colleagues. After all, I did not have

a PH.D. This reminded me of my earlier years with my brothers. I really miss them. My

family had all predeceased me.

Anyhow, my brother Pat enlisted in the navy and was a "Sea Bee". My thinking was

that studying a trade was worse than going to school simply because you have to get

your hands dirty. I was not into fixing cars, or cutting grass, or anything that required me

to get my hands dirty. Who, I would think to myself, in their right mind would want to

do that? Surely, this type of work was not me. There had to be a better way. Work?

Wow, work is a four-letter word requiring manual labor, I thought. I could not

stand the thought literally or figuratively. Ah, I was young and did not have a clue.

I see that today in many of the younger students. They are no different than I was back

then. Sure, they are more sophisticated regarding social media and technology, but that

is the only difference. We just lived in a different time.

I started grade school in a parochial school in Meriden, Connecticut, called

Saint Laurent School. I remember having the sisters as our teachers. I remember the

priests also comprising a large part of our education. My memory is clear regarding my

grade school days. Fathers Matthew and Perrault were our priests. I also recall the

respect we all had for our teachers. For some reason, as I think back, I recall how we

were afraid of the parish priests. Despite our fear, we had a profound respect for them.

In fact, when Father Matthew would call me over, I specifically remember always

saying in almost a rehearsed way: "Good Morning, Father," and "How are you today?" I

never recall anyone ever being disrespectful to Father Matthew, Perrault, or any of

the Sisters. If anything, we were taught to respect these people more than we

respected our own parents. I believe there was a fear generated by their very presence. In

any event, the entire student body was joined and unified in that fear. I laugh when I

think about it today because there really was no reason to fear. These religious figures

were truly wonderful people. They were the best type of role models. They were strict

and no-nonsense types. They always took our best interests to heart. That fact is the

truth. My church and school experience while at St. Laurent was truly a beautiful and

wonderful experience. I cannot say one bad thing about it. My education made me a better person. I am proud of it and believe the religious aspect had a positive impact.

Father Matthew was elderly and was always holding his heart. My first grade teacher was Sister Veronica who must have been in her eighties. I recall her smile and the way she always walked very quickly. She looked like a little penguin because she was so short. She was such a nice lady. She never raised her voice to anyone. She had the power of the "look". If she looked at you a certain way, you knew you were in trouble-big trouble. Her eyes would pierce through you. When Sister looked at you that way, you would be stunned as if you turned to stone for that moment. She had a very unique way about her. She was old but never came across as acting old. It was like the Lord blessed her with "youth" for the purpose of caring for us. No one ever thought of this Sister as being old. I never could understand that though. She was our teacher.

She was always a dedicated teacher. She kept our classroom spotless. I seem to recall her always cleaning or grading papers, or simply always being busy for some odd reason. She, like the other sisters, were never idle that I could recall. She was always smiling. She never seemed to let anything get her down. She was an angel. She was happy, hardworking, dedicated, and spiritual. We all loved her.

I understand how truly fortunate I was to have attended St. Laurent. Despite constant criticism of Catholic Schools today, even criticism lodged by my daughter, I learned a profound respect for the people who taught and guided me. I can recall things occurring back then with such clarity. This is incredible since many of these memories go back to the early 1960s or about fifty-seven years ago. I cannot recall what I had for dinner yesterday, but I can recall these memories with such specificity. I would often ask my students in class if they could recall their earliest memories. Put another way, what is the earliest point they could recall growing up. I would inquire how old they were at the time of their recollection and what specifically they recalled. (I can recall sitting on my mother's lap. I kept trying to get off her lap to stand. When she would put me down to stand, I would fall over. We were on a plane to Nova Scotia, and I was a little over one year old). In my case, I could recall quite a way back.

For example, in second or third grade, I can recall my class getting an older student, John, who was held back. I believe I was seven at the time. John, by his being held back was a bit older and somewhat bigger than the rest of the boys in our class. Some of the girls were his size though. John was a good kid, but could not sit still to save his life. He was full of energy and not afraid to show off or to start a fight because of his size. He would often bully the older kids in the higher grades. I remember that fact quite vividly. He tried bullying me, but I was simply not afraid of John. After all, he was in my class. I simply figured that what goes around comes around. If he messed with me, I would have the chance to mess with him at some point. So, if he chased me, I simply ignored him and did not run. I guess that caught John off guard. He realized I was not afraid of him, so he stopped bothering me.

Regarding class, John needed medication by today's standards. Well needless to say, the Sisters had their own kind of medicine which they would use to deal with what they considered to be obnoxious or uncooperative behavior. I recall one day in particular when John kept making noises in class, and Sister Catherine, I believe, attempted to deal

27

with him. First, the Sister asked John nicely to behave. That request by the Sister should have ended the problem. Well, John was persistent and kept it up. He simply would not listen.

I recall Sister asking the student in the first row right in front of her desk to move, and then telling John to sit there right in front ("where I can see you", she said). I guess Sister thought she could keep an eye on John and this would make him behave. Well, it was a noble effort but it simply did not work. I remember how John smiled, and changed seats as directed. It was a devilish grin. I think John loved the special attention he was getting. When Sister Catherine would turn her back to write something on the black board, John would mock her by making a foolish gesture in turn making the entire class laugh. (You must remember that sister wore that black robe kind of thing, which made it difficult for her to reach up to write on the board. Sister would have to raise her arm once, and then again, and even then, again because of the heavy cloth she was wearing. I can picture it in my mind as she strained to reach up and to simply write on the black board). As Sister turned around with her back to us, John would mock her gestures. When Sister would turn around again or look back at the class, she looked at John who would appear to be sitting there in his seat attentively tapping his fingers on his chin as if he were pensively trying to understand the lesson. ("Ya Right!", I would say to my-self.) Well, sister was no fool and she immediately saw through John's antics and told John to move back a seat telling the student in that seat to move back. Ah, John thought to himself as he smiled that Sister is giving up and I've won this one. I thought to myself again "Ya right". There was no way Sister was giving up that easily. "Poor John"-everyone in the class thought knowing the situation clearly better than John realized. I thought to myself: "Gee, a sucker is born every minute".

There were five or six seats per row. John continued to the second seat in the row as sister cleared that entire row for John alone almost like a fortune teller predicting the future. Whenever sister would turn her back, John would make a noise or some type of mocking gesture as a distraction which clearly annoyed sister and tested her angelic/ saintly patience. (I am not sure whether sister had the patience of a saint back on that occasion but am simply giving her the benefit of the doubt).

Within a half hour, John was now sitting in the back seat of the row with no other place to go. I guess sister had in fact predicted the future. Sister then made a point to warn John again, telling him that he has run out of seats. As Sister would turn her back once again, John would continue to mock her behind her back. The plot thickened as the class continued to laugh each time. Now, keep in mind that Sister wore a black dress with a type of black and white head cover with a white-like bib. Her face then turned bright red, and with the black robe and head covering, well, I must tell you this contrast made me see the colors of the devil (absent the horns). I was not the most observant student, but this black and red vision had to mean something bad was going to happen. I knew that and in fact, I think everybody knew that except John. It was a bad omen and not an Amen like we say after a prayer. (Like Oh man, what next?)

There was no doubt in my mind that Satan was in that classroom. The only problem was how to determine who he was influencing, John or Sister or the class? Sister warned

29

John but one last time: "John, this is the last time I am warning you to stop and pay attention, or else"? As she spoke, sister continued to the far back end of the classroom, and by now annoyed, she opened the fire-escape door. Hum, I noticed and heard that it was raining cats and dogs. I could not understand why Sister opened the door, but she had her reasons none the less. Perhaps she was being influenced by the Holy Spirit, who is that third-person of the Holy Trinity who is supposed to inspire wisdom in times of need. The problem I was having was I could not figure out who needed the inspiration most, was it John, Sister, or the Class? I simply could not tell then, nor could I tell today. Perhaps she was being influenced by the devil, I do not know. I still remember the rain pouring down from the door as I see it all so clearly in my mind. The rain was not entering the classroom thank God. I could smell and see and feel it. (I don't think it rains in hell!)

It looked like the Great Flood all over again but I was not betting on any Rainbows. Sister Catherine looked at John and said, "the next peep out of you John, and you will find yourself sitting out in the rain". Well, as fate would have it, John continued to mock Sister whenever she would turn her back. He just would not heed the clear, precise warnings given him. God knows he was given plenty of warnings. As Sister turned her back once again, John yelled "peep-peep-peep" as loud has he could and stamped his foot on the floor. The entire class roared. Sister turned bright, bright red like a boiled lobster. It was almost like the fires of hell had scorched her face, and this was not a holy sign. (It was more like Holy Shit!) I envisioned the Fires of Hell in our classroom.

Sister immediately stopped her writing on the board, as if there was some sort of divine intervention. I then assume as I recall- the Holy Spirit coming unto Sister Catherine; It was like a light-bulb had gone off in her head. She was truly inspired. You know the look when someone seems to get an idea-how he/she appears to be enlightened. Well, that was it, sister got inspired for sure. Maybe it was the Third Person who inspired her. Maybe it was someone else who inspired her. I really don't think it was the Father or the Son, but I hope it was at the very least the Holy Ghost. Sister turned around to look at us, and within a moment she then approached John, and told him to stand up. She grabbed John's desk, proceeded to pick it up and then carried it out onto the wet fire-escape. It was a miracle. As Sister carried the desk out onto the fire-escape, she did not get wet. The rains parted and circumvented her. It was like the parting of the Red Sea. Sister then came in and smiled, as if possessed by you-know-who, and ordered John to sit in the desk out on the fire-escape while it continued to poured cats and dogs. "Gee", I thought to myself, "the Holy Spirit works in such mysterious ways". I hope it was the Holy Spirit, because it could have been someone else working in a more clandestine way. John did as Sister demanded and sat in the chair outside on the fire-escape while it continued to pour by now Tigers and Bears. I figured that Sister would make John sit out there for a few moments and then would allow him back into the dry classroom once he started to behave. I suppose Sister simply wanted to make her point to John and to the class. As the rain continued to fall, John decided that he would simply not give in. He started stomping his hands and feet making the water splash causing more of a ruckus than before. Well, it was like a true Divine Order or Epiphany from

God, because by now Sister Catherine had had it and was intent on leaving John outside to be again Baptized this time in the Creative Grace of God. There was no doubt that John was truly showered with the Grace of God that day through his newly acquired wisdom; Don't mess with Sister Catherine. As John splashed, Sister simply shut the fire escape door. Anyhow, no one from that day forward messed with our Sister Catherine again, to my knowledge. We all had learned a lesson from John's antics. The Sisters of Saint Laurent are blessed disciples of God. When you mess with them, you mess with God. I'd rather take my chances with my parents. This was a true story then and is a true story now.

Now one other story comes to mind. I was in the third grade at the time. I was about nine or ten years old. One day at school, I noticed that a few of my classmates were wearing torn shirts and pants. I approached one of them to ask what happened. The classmate said, "Did they get you too"? I looked at him and simply did not understand what in God's world he was talking about. I went about my day not thinking too much about it.

Later, I noticed a group of fifth graders chasing one of my classmates. I also noticed that as they caught him, they were hitting and spitting on him. I quickly intervened pulling a few of the fifth graders off my friend. Needless to say, once I intervened, that caused a counter-reaction whereby the entire fifth grade class (the boys) started to hitting me. I proceeded to run as quickly as I could to get away. At that time, I was one of the fastest runners in my class. I would run, weave and dodge the fifth graders. Most of the boys in the fifth grade were bigger and some fatter than I was. As I proceeded to run and dodge and weave in between the fifth-grade boys, I would reach out and pull on their shirts ripping them. When all was said and done, the boys never caught me, but the entire class had all torn shirts when we proceeded back to classes. I was simply happy that I could get away from them all prior to the bell ringing.

About a half hour after class started, someone knocked on our class door giving a message to our teacher. It was a student from the fifth grade. Evidently, Sister Agnes sent the student to my class to ask the teacher to have me report to her (Sister Agnes's class). My teacher then stated "Francis", (my patron saint's name), "Sister Agnes would like to see you". I got up and proceeded upstairs to the fifth-grade classroom and knock-ed on the door.

Sister Agnes had me come in and as I entered, I noticed all the boys with torn shirts smiling at me as I entered. Well needless to say, Sister Agnes was angry. She apparently was upset because all her boys had ripped shirts. There was not one boy in that class that did not have a severely torn shirt on. Sister looked at me and said "Did you do all this?" I smiled. "Sister" I said, "look at me". "I am probably half the size of these boys". "They, all of them, were chasing and hitting the boys in the third grade". "They could not catch me". As I spoke, I looked at the fifth-grade boys and saw their smiles dwindle after I spoke. Sister Agnes told me that I should pay for all their shirts. I responded "Yes Sister" and simply smiled. As I left and shut the door, I could then hear Sister Agnes saying "You ought to be ashamed of yourselves. You let that shrimp get the best of you-shame on you". I laughed as I ran down the stairs to my classroom. "Ah, the thrill of victory, and the agony of defeat" I said to myself. Those fifth graders never bullied me or my classmates again. You see, there really is a God. I confess that I ripped about three of the fifth-graders shirts, but when I was called into the fifth grade class, all of the fifteen or twenty boys had ripped shirts. God punished them. They all got together ripping each others' shirts to try to make me look bad. It back fired when Sister Agnes scolded them. She did not believe that I had done all that they said I had.

The reason I mention this is simple: there are a few observations that I need to make. Catholic School taught me to read and write. I read slowly but did in fact learn to read and write well. I learned respect for my teachers as John's lesson clearly illustrates. Respect was learned one way or another. We learned this the easy way, or if not, we learned this the hard way. Please note, we did learn it though. The end result was the same: Respect.

When I graduated high school, I recall telling my father that I wanted to go to college but was not sure what major to pursue. He asked me what I thought I would be interested in studying. I thought I wanted to go to law school. His response was that I had better get my grades up because my high school grades were not very good. I knew he was right. I took his advice to heart and started to work hard.

I took the SATS and got accepted to the University of Connecticut. I majored in Political Science and entered the Honors Program thinking that I might be better able to compete for a law school spot. I did work hard while at UConn, and I did quite well.

My father kept telling me to focus on my grades and to do well. He really did inspire me. He did so in the following ways: 1. Dad always told me to work hard and to never give up. If you set your aim towards a particular goal, work hard to achieve that goal. 2. Dad always told me to do my best, and never think that any job is below me. 3. Dad always told me to respect others in order to earn respect. 4. Dad always told me that no matter what the job or position is, if done well, the efforts generate respect. It could be a janitor for example or any job for that matter. When the boss recognizes a person who works hard, no matter what the job is, the boss will view that person as vital to the operation and protect that person even when other managers or higher ups disagree. He will go out of his way to protect that employee from the vultures. I was told never to forget that. 5. Dad always told me never to look down upon anyone, and never to think I am better than anyone else. The key to success, according to my father, was simply to try to be fair to and understanding of others. He always reminded me that not everyone is born with an entire or complete deck of cards. Always appreciate that fact and always try to alleviate his/her load and try to make the deck fair. If you are fortunate enough to have success that should mean to you that you are fortunate enough to share that success with others. Always try your best to help people who are less fortunate and who are in need. Never turn your back on others when you can help. Your efforts will truly reward you. Your success or lack thereof always comes from the grace of God, and just as soon as you have success, so too can you lose it. Be mindful of this. Be the best person you can be. It does not matter who you end up being or becoming. Always try to be a good person first above all else. Try to remember that, and if you do, all else will fall into place. I can remember those words dad often shared with me. He was always honest and sincere. My father never lied to me. This was my "Dad". He was a good man.

I never realized how important those things were until he died. Boy do I know now. Despite his sixth-grade education, my dad knew quite a bit. In fairness, I always knew it but sometimes did not appreciate it. At least I learned to appreciate it later. Learning to appreciate something or someone, even if late, is better than never learning to do so.

My father also commented that if and when I graduate and find a job that I truly like, to always remember that upon that occurring, I would truly be blessed by God. I heard him, but did not listen to him. How many times do we hear but not listen? I simply remember thinking, "ya, ya, ya". Those were some of the earlier memories that I fondly recall.

Chapter Three:

"A Jealous Mistress- Really"?

I thought that my dream was to become a lawyer and to practice law. I therefore pursued a Political Science Degree with the hope of becoming a practicing attorney. I thought that by taking some undergraduate law classes I would surely prepare my-self for law school. The law classes were fun, but nothing like the real thing in law school. I later learned that the law schools actually prefer that students take their law courses at their law school, and stay away from similar classes while pursuing an undergraduate degree. Despite doing well at the University of Connecticut, I later realized that law school was a whole different ballgame. I always tell my old and new students that law school is so much different from undergraduate studies. They always ask me to explain how law school differs from undergraduate school.

When I attended my first-year contract law class, the professor looked at all of us, and very bluntly said: "Hi, welcome to law school. Kindly take a look around, and see how many of you are in this class. Please note the number as I am sure you are aware there are now quite a few of you present. Now, the reason I say this is that by this time next year, half of you will not be here". I knew immediately what he meant. He simply was communicating a known fact to all of us. The fact is simply that the law is a "jealous mistress". If any of the students in class are not truly committed to the study of law, they simply won't be here this time next year. I heard it time and time again. The message continues to go on like this: If you have small children at home, you should stay home and enjoy your children while they are growing up. If you try to attend classes and enjoy your children, something will have to give. If you are married and attending law school, your wife or husband will have to understand that he/she comes in second to the rigorous study of law. The law again is a jealous mistress. This was/is always a hard but a true fact to understand and to accept.

So, what is the difference between undergrad and grad studies? I would always tell my students that law school is more like participating in athletics. If you were ever on a team, like in high school, your actual performance was based upon practice and achievement (through practice). Law School was and is, just like participating in sports/ athletics. There is truly little to study in terms of rote memory. When asked by my students despite my teaching in the Political Science Department for so many years, what is the best type of preparation in terms of course of study for law, I hesitatingly would answer the study of a foreign language. The case book readings in law school whereby the student must brief each case closely equates with what students do when they go through the mental process of translation. For example, when a student reads a case in law school, he/she must (or at least is expected to) brief the case. The process of briefing a case is like translation to the foreign language and Vice-Versa. I am quite clear on this because I took French in high school. The two mental acts are the same. Students must summarize the facts, procedure, and creatively craft the issue of the case. He/she must then answer the issue, and determine the relevant public policies of the case. It is a process the student learns by continually reading and writing more briefs. The more practice one has, the better one becomes. This is like athletics. If you are diver, the more dives you practice, the better you become. If you are a swimmer, once you have mastered your stroke or strokes, the more laps you swim, the better your strokes and your endurance become. Briefing cases, like swimming laps, or running marathons, is a grueling and difficult process. It is arduous and once the student gets a hang of it, it forces the student to synthesize his/her thoughts. As the student becomes better with his/her briefs, he/she notices a shorter, better discreet work of art if you will. The two-dimensional page becomes a multidimensional work including the facts, the procedure, the issue, the holding, and the public policies of the case. The piece of paper becomes a real, working legal case. What first appears to be abstract in many ways becomes real and practical. If the student understands the case, his/her brief will indicate that comprehension. If the student fails to understand the case, his/her brief will indicate that lack of comprehension and confusion. This is how it works.

The process is hard to master. Some people, including law graduates and even practicing lawyers, never really master it at all. Tough things are never really fun. Law School is not fun. It is not meant to be fun either. Undergraduate school is often a lot of fun. As stated, this process forces students to analyze and synthesize facts and law in such a way that it is called legal analysis or simply "thinking like a lawyer". The law school professors call it thinking like a lawyer and it is a learned process which comes easier to some but harder to many. I always tell my students practice counts but short cuts do not count. Law Schools teach this grueling process. Law students must learn it or attempt to get a handle on it as best they can.

Keep in mind that learning to think like a lawyer is only part of the equation. In class, the professor will call on students to brief the case. The student, at least at my law school, would have to stand and have all of the work completed to be able to answer some/most of the professor's questions. The student must be prepared, organized, articulate and confident. Although students in undergraduate school learn some of these things, normally when they attend the first year of law school they are quite traumatized to say the least. If you have a tough law professor, the trauma or shock is compounded.

The basic law school class includes use of the Socratic Method. The teacher will ask a series of questions to try to ascertain whether the student understands the legal concepts of the case at hand. This resembles a baby crawling. First, the student must read the case and understand the facts. This is the simple part of it all. If the student cannot understand the facts, then he/she will have problems understanding the case. Facts are important because once read and understood, the student can learn to reason by analogy when he/she sees similar fact patterns in cases that arise later. The study of these facts train legal minds to learn to manipulate and creatively implement the facts to different scenarios. This is what lawyers do. There is no rote memory.

For example, let me explain. The teacher will call on a student. Let us pretend the student's name is Paul. Now Paul is an older student, who probably is thirty-five or so, and has decided to attend law school after his son aged a bit. Paul applied to law school, had a 3.8 grade point average, and scored in the top ten percent on his LSAT.

The professor calls on Paul, who stands and proceeds to brief the case the Professor requests him to brief. As Paul starts with the facts, the Professor will interrupt loudly to ask Paul about certain specific facts about the case. As long as Paul answers the questions correctly, the Professor will keep questioning him. If Paul misses a question, which typically occurs after the first or second question, the Professor will then move on to someone else. Please note, though, the Professor will mark down that he/she has called on Paul, and move on to someone else on the attendance roster until all students are eventually called upon in this way.

If Paul is not prepared, the Professor will often embarrass him. This occurs in the movie "The Paper Chase" when Professor Kingsfield (John Houseman) calls on Mr. James T. Hart (Timothy Bottoms) and Mr. Hart tells Kingsfield he hadn't read the case. Kingsfield proceeds to call Hart to the podium, and gives him a dime telling him to call his mother to tell her he will not be (able) to become a lawyer. Hart proceeds back to his seat, and as he proceeds to leave the classroom, calls Kingsfield a "son-of-a-bitch". Kingsfield responded, "that is the most intelligent thing you or anyone in this class has said this evening," and tells Hart to "take your seat". The point is that every law school has its own version of a Kingsfield. There is always that one professor who is simply like Kingsfield. It does not matter where you go, or what law school you attend. He/she truly exists everywhere.

Keep in mind that when Paul messes up, every other student gauges his/her perform-ance based upon Paul's performance. The student determines whether he/she could have answered as many if not more, or less questions, than Paul answered. If Paul answered more of the Professor's questions than let's say, I would have been able to answer, then I would try harder to improve my study habits so next time I could and would answer more questions. Further, keep in mind that the Professor will take a student one at a time from his/her roster. So, if I am not called on today, I could be called on tomorrow or at least when the class next meets. For those law students who cannot seem to ever answer any of the professor's questions, they become despondent and question their ability to be in law school. Many students will drop out. Some students will flunk out, while others' will quit, or will even contemplate (or commit) suicide.

Further, when the professor calls on a student and the student says something wrong, or stupid, if you will, the entire class will often laugh and raise their hands. The point is that the competition is fierce. Every law student wants to be the model student in front of the professor and his/her peers. The entire law school experience is mind-boggling. It is very unique and competitive. The students do not mean anything by laughing, but it surely hurts the student trying his or her best only to be laughed at and ridiculed in class. I try to tell this to my students. I often get peer pressure from colleagues not to scare the students away. I really don't mean to do that. I do intend to let my students know the reality of the situation. Most of my colleagues who have not been there, or who have not done it, are simply unaware. It is a grueling process only to be possibly rivaled by the medical schools. I truly mean what I say and am not joking about this. I have also been told that it is very different from the PH.D programs. I suppose the Juris Doctorate is more of a diversified degree while the PH.D is more of a specified degree.

In my thirty years at Southern, I have never witnessed this. Southern classes I teach or taught were mostly undergraduate classes with a few hybrid classes mixed in here and there. The graduate classes are a bit tougher than the undergraduate classes as should be expected. I suppose these are the things mentioned that I believe are the ways law school differ from undergraduate school. What is scary though is the fact that if you ask any lawyer about my comments, you will see that most attorneys, if not all, will agree with what I say. The study of law is simply very difficult and time consuming. Without a firm commitment to legal studies, one should simply not attend.

I mention this because when students say they want to go to law school, I really don't think they know the type of commitment they are undertaking. I firmly believe that when I hear that statement, that unless the student has a burning desire to succeed, that they are just huffing and puffing and nothing else. I recall many of my students who decided to go on to law school and who later called me often in a state of panic. I recall talking to him/her and trying to calm him/her down. Every one of these students have admitted to me that it (legal studies) is so much different from their undergraduate studies. Despite many of these students having high grade point averages, they all admitted that law school was something entirely different from what they imagined. Not one student ever told me that it was easy. Not one ever told me it was a cake walk. Not a single student has ever told me it was a breeze. Most students have firmly stated or admitted to me the fact that I was right about their legal studies. All have stated it is not fun. It was and is simply hard work. This fact cannot be stressed enough.

I must be fair to the undergraduate curriculum. One exception exists to include the benefit students obtain from receiving a liberal arts education. By majoring in liberal arts, the student takes a variety of courses that law schools believe better prepare him/her for the different law classes. Also, I am told that older students often make better law students simply because of their life experiences. Evidently the longer a student lives, the more familiar he/she is with mortgages, credit, business, life, and the better equipped he/she is for the study of law. I believe this to be true. This is a proven fact and evidenced by the high admission rate among older students and their high graduation rate from law schools.

Some of my students have asked about the LSAT and whether it truly predicts student success in the first year. I believe it does. Today, the question may actually be moot in some respects. When I applied to law school the LSAT was a requirement. Students today can get around this requirement. For example, if a student does not test well, he/she can apply to the Massachusetts School of Law in Andover. The Law School is not ABA approved, but for Connecticut residents, if they pass their three years there, they then are able to sit for the Connecticut and Massachusetts' Bars. Evidently the school entered into an agreement with the Connecticut Bar Examining Committee allowing its graduates to sit for the Bar in this state. Of course, if the student wants to attend Harvard or Yale, or another prestigious school, he/she will have to pursue the traditional route of graduating from an undergraduate institution (fully credited), then of sitting for the LSAT, (receive an acceptable score), and then of being admitted to an ABA-approved law school. It is a lesson in perseverance and nothing else. I say this because if a student performs poorly on the LSAT and if he/she attends a poorly rated ABA-approved law school, he/she after passing his/her first year can then transfer to a better rated law school. As you are aware, not everyone can get into Yale or Harvard Law School.

Students can also pursue legal education in California. California has the largest number of non-ABA approved law schools in the country, and there one can become a lawyer by simply passing the California Bar. California is supposed to have one of the hardest Bars in the country. The California Bar Examiner mentality is simple. In California, the thinking goes, if you pass the Bar, you are an attorney. It is as simple as that. The Bar Examining Committee does not care if you read the law, take an on line or correspondence course in the law, or proceed however which way you like. If you pass their Bar, you are a California attorney. Of course, I am sure passing is not all that easy. I knew a Professor from California, named William Lynch. Bill was a Judge Advocate in the Military, and practiced law in Massachusetts for over twenty years. He was hired as a law professor at the California Western School of Law in San Diego. Well, when Bill arrived in California, he thought he would take the Bar for the heck of it. Needless to say, Bill got his score back with a zero on the essay section. (I believe it was on one portion or the other, as I cannot recall really). I remember Bill telling me that if that wasn't a blow to his ego, nothing was. Can you imagine being a practicing attorney for over twenty years, and doing so poorly on a State Bar exam. Bill then took a Bar Review course offered in California and passed with flying colors.

I also receive questions from students about the law school ratings. How, does Harvard Law School differ from one of the brand new recently accredited ABA

Law Schools. First of all, students with perfect credentials often apply to Yale and Harvard. Some of those applicants get rejected. I always tell my students that even if someone with perfect credentials gets rejected from the school of his/her choice, he/she still gets in somewhere and attends. Newer law schools do not have established reputations because the school has not been in existence long enough to get its graduates out there. These newer schools are often much easier to get into. One caveat exists. Just because someone gets accepted does not mean he/she will graduate. New schools will try to improve their reputations. Often, they do this by accepting new students but flunking out many of them. My point is that even the newer schools will have a rigorous curriculum. The first-year classes are all the same. No matter where a student attends, he/she will have to take the following first year classes: Criminal Law; Contracts; Torts; Civil Procedure; Legal Research and Writing (possibly criminal procedure).

Any further analysis of the law school curriculum is for another day. Suffice it to say simply that in the past one could become an attorney by simply reading the law and working with an attorney. By the late eighteen hundreds, the legal profession became formalized or professionalized by a rigorous curriculum prepared by judges and practicing attorneys. Today, we have a basic three-year curriculum after college. As everyone knows, the first year is the same no matter where you go. The first year is the hardest. If you fail in the first year, the "fact of failure is your first year".

Can the current program be improved? I am sure it can. Will it? I simply do not think so. Why? Lawyers are often great thinkers, but often poor administrators and educators. For example, in the early sixties and seventies, many law schools did not require its students to take Constitutional Law. It was not until the ABA required law schools to mandate this class did many law schools comply. I cite this as an example because law students, once they pass their State Bar, must take an oath to support and defend the constitution of the United States. How does a student, in good conscience, take that oath without ever having taken the class - constitutional law? How does a law school know this and still fail to mandate the course? Do you see what I mean? This is simply not believable. Who should know better about the legal process than the law school deans? Most attorneys feel that if the current curriculum is not broken, it should be left alone. There you have it, plain and simple. The way the law schools avoid the static argument is by the administrators' position that they maintain most of the legal internships and clerkships which keep the students/professors abreast of current trends and needs in the community, the state, and the nation. Further, with active law reviews, the law schools often offer symposiums to educate the public on recent legal trends. Most Law School Deans would argue their schools perform a vital legal/educational function in society. In that way and in some respects, the current law school curriculum is therefore dynamic and here to stay. I do not buy that argument. There is always a better approach. The current thinking is static, but because the law itself is evolving, the schools must offer newer courses to stay competitive. The instruction though, depending on the professor, can still be static. I keep hearing the same argument, if static works, then leave it alone. This reminds me of the static you hear on the radio. It simply annoys me. There is much work to be done to improve the current law school curriculum. Tough economic times together with lower applications and enrollments make this a back-burner issue at present.

Chapter Four:
"My Undergraduate Studies - A Blessing or a Curse?"

My college days were from 1973-1977. Things were a lot different in those days. Many of us recall the 1973 OPEC oil embargo. I remember gas prices before graduating from high school being $.39/9 at our local Hess Gas station. Almost overnight, with the Oil Embargo, prices rose from $.39/9 to almost $2.00. I can recall gas lines with these rising prices; I can recall gas rationing only permitting gas purchases based upon having even and odd license plates. It was a mess. Inflation soared.

Not too much unlike today, we all had our economic challenges we had to endure. The economy seemed a bit better in those days, but my recollection then was surely not a mature recollection as I was eighteen and viewed society through a myopic lens. I was selfish, and thought the world revolved around me. We all have been there and have experience with that mentality. It exists today.

Even as late as 1973, though, our state still had a lot of factory positions. Our state of Connecticut, like many states, had not evolved from an industrial to a service-oriented economy yet. We still experienced remnants of unlimited growth. Well, I suppose visions of it existed anyhow. Change was inevitable.

I attended the University of Connecticut. Although I had received notice that I was placed on the waiting list at Yale, I decided to attend UConn and am glad I went there. I can recall listening to basketball games with the other students in the dorm, and recall how UConn was a good choice. It was huge in terms of its physical plant, keeping in mind that when a student first arrives on campus little does he/she know about the massive buildings including dorms and acreage. Back when I attended, the University still had a large student population. Although many of the students commuted to Storrs, many others lived minutes away from campus housed in private apartments. I stayed in the dorms on campus.

When I took my first political science course, I had a professor named Henry Krisch for Comparative Politics. Henry was a great guy, from Columbia, and had black curly hair. I recently saw him at Dr. Gerson's memorial service held on the Storrs campus. He really had not changed much over the past forty-three years. I commented to him that I could not understand how he still had all his hair. He smiled and asked me about a colleague of mine at Southern, Dr. Paul Best. I told him Paul was fine and also mentioned that I would give Paul his "best" regards. I did that at our monthly meeting of retirees. (I am retired now, and only work part time.)

Henry chose a book that was really dry. Out of fairness though, this was not just my opinion. Dr. Krisch also commented in class a few times that the book even annoyed him in that regard. I credit Henry with always trying to keep the class alive. He was always very motivated and up-beat in class. He always called on students who had questions, and always tried to address those questions in a way that was not demeaning or condescending to students. I liked that about Dr. Krisch. He made you feel at ease with him in his class. I truly admired him as a teacher. He generated a warmth which made everyone enjoy his class. I clearly enjoyed his class.

Now as an aside, I was not aware at the time that I was so critical of my professors.

To this day, I think of it as a blessing in that it amounts to constructive criticism, but also as a curse because it picks away at teachers who are often good people who try their very best. I often wish that I was not this way but my mind works in a critical way. I learned a vital lesson at that time: If I were ever to teach a class, I would make sure the book is at least tolerable for me and for my students. I suppose that this is part of the planning for the class. It is the "due diligence" if you will. It is part of the idea that the teacher is well-prepared and is setting a good example. He/she should also be following the boy scout motto of "always be prepared". THIS WAS LESSON ONE.

Further, Henry liked science fiction books and assigned two Robert Heinlein books as part of the course. I really think Professor Krisch did this to relieve the tension and provide students with something enjoyable. Like beauty, joy too, is in the eye of the beholder. Henry gets an "A" from me for effort. Unfortunately, I hated science fiction books then, and I hate them now. I learned another vital lesson: If I were ever to teach a class, I promised myself that I would never, ever, force my hobbies on my students. As I stated before, these good intentions get an "A" for effort, but that is about it. I enjoy suspense books. For example, I enjoy the "master of suspense" Alfred Hitchcock. I suppose I could assign a bunch of stories Hitchcock chose to base his movies on. How does "Psycho" sound? Well, I am sure it does not sound all that great at the moment. I like time travel, and spent time reading Stephen Hawking's "A Brief History of Time". I suppose I could assign that book for the section on time travel. Most of my students would think "ya, maybe I could use it to travel as far from this class as humanly possible". I think you get my drift. I simply do not think it fair to use my authority as a teacher to force my hobby down the throats of my students. I would call this simply an "abuse of my official authority" and would never do this. Many people would probably disagree with me. THIS WAS LESSON TWO.

I also noticed while at UConn that the teachers would assign sometimes up to four or five books per class. I believe this was done primarily to keep students busy since they were on campus and really did have plenty of time to get their assignments done. (Keep in mind that this statement refers to students living on campus). I think the Professors simply wanted the students to learn a lot in their classes. Hence, there was this pile-it-on mentality. This was OK, as long as the books were actually used in the classroom. What I noticed occurring was that many of the Professors assigned many of the books as optional readings without clearly articulating that fact on the syllabus. I don't know if that has ever happened to you. You go to the book store, see the required readings for let us say Professor Smart-al-lick, and then attempt to buy all of the books. You get the syllabus and notice all the books are marked "required reading" for the class. So, if you did not buy all the books your first trip to the book store, you go back to buy them because the Professor's syllabus tells you to do so. The listed books are required reading.

I learned that it was always best to inquire or ask the professor prior to buying every book listed. I don't know if the teachers did this to trick the students or not. I did know then, and I do know now, that no one wants to buy books he/she does not need. I state this because my daughter, Eva- Anne, was told to purchase a book that the Professor did not use. The book was very expensive. I could not believe that a teacher would do this. My colleagues refrain from doing this. It simply makes no sense.

Today when I decide to assign books to my students, I think back to those UConn days to try to be cognizant of my students' concerns. I would always try to be fair and never strain vital student resources. I think that this comment is universally true. I know that all my colleagues are on board with this.

Anyhow, that was my first political science course at UConn and God knows how close I came to majoring in "Puppetry" because of these things mentioned. I learned that if I were ever to teach a class, that I would utilize every effort to keep the class interesting. I always thought that by being a little creative I could go a long way to achieving this goal. I learned firsthand that this type of preparation would help make the class "Dynamic" and not "Static". Henry's choice of a dry book hurt his class. I thought I was going to die trying to read that book. I always kept a good/positive attitude, but questioned my interest in the subject matter after taking this class. This was not good. Should I stay in Political Science? I was not sure. After all, I told my dad I wanted to major in political science. I simply felt that if I told dad I changed my mind, he would think of me as a quitter. Oh gosh, I did not want that. This bothered me because I did not want to attend college to simply waste my time. I did not want to attend college just to get a piece of paper. I was at a real cross-road.

This was not a good feeling and brought about a type of soul searching. It haunted me. Henry tried to bring real world events into the class room discussion, but these efforts did not seem to change my mind. I was frustrated with political science.

I simply was not fair to Henry because I did not know much about him prior to taking his class. I did not know, for instance, how long he taught at the time. I guess I could have done some research on my own prior to taking the class. I cannot blame Henry for my shortcomings either. Fairness is a two-way street. I was partly to blame. For all I knew, this class could have been Henry's first class. Maybe he never taught a class prior to this one. I also did not understand at the time that had the department made a last minute course change, Henry could have been stuck with the book choice made from someone else. Thus, I guess to be fair, Henry did a fine job and I probably should have done my due diligence prior to taking his class.

I told myself, if I were ever to teach a class, I would keep the information up-to-date and discuss current events to emphasize the importance of the material to the present. Students need to recognize that their learning material is relevant. They need to understand how vital their education is to their life and future. Things discussed and seen in the news media help keep students interested and motivated. This makes students participate in class. This further helps the teacher keep the course alive and dynamic. Only the teacher is responsible for course presentation. The buck really does stop there. THIS WAS LESSON THREE.

I was annoyed with Henry because I felt he made us buy books we did not need. This was at a cost to the students. Most of the students I knew simply did not have much money. I told myself, if I were ever to teach a class, I would shop around for a text book that was not too expensive in an effort to keep the costs down for my students. I would inquire whether the book could be ordered in paperback as opposed to hardcover. I told myself that I would not assign books unnecessarily for the class. I might consider assigning other books for extra credit assignments or for term papers and the like. Also, if I did assign outside books, I would place a copy of each book on reserve at the library for students at no cost to them. If I were to assign a book as the class textbook that seemed too expensive or was in fact expensive, I would always place a copy or two on reserve for those students who simply could not afford the text. I did try to make things a bit easier for my students in that regard. Most of my students clearly appreciated my effort. THIS WAS LESSON FOUR.

Sometimes the publishers would send our Department more than one copy of a textbook. Sometimes my colleagues would have copies of a text book they simply were not using. In some cases where a student was awaiting his/her financial aid and was unable to purchase a book, I would take the liberty to loan a book out as long as it was not a teacher's edition. I would always remind my students that if they chose not to buy the text book, they could always go to the library and read the book on reserve at their leisure. The only pitfall with this option was the fact that these reserve texts were only permitted for library use and were not for home use. (Reserve material for library use only.) Today with the unique convenience of renting text books either by way of the internet or by way of hard copy, many of the issues I experienced are no longer present. It is fair to say that cost should always be an issue and should be considered and dealt with appropriately by the teacher whenever possible. This concern should always be a motivating factor in the teacher's text selection.

I was asked by a student why the texts are not included in the price of tuition? I laughed. I thought to myself - "ya sure". Teaching so long has in some instances blinded me. If you really think about it, I don't know why the books could not be included in the tuition. Perhaps, at some time soon, someone will wake up and do this. It really is a good idea. Unfortunately, I simply do not see it happening.

A Corollary to lessons one through four above is:

> NEVER, EVER, ASSIGN MATERIALS YOU DON'T INTEND TO USE. THIS FOSTERS DISRESPECT AS STUDENTS STRUGGLE TO COMPREHEND WHY A PROFESSOR IN COLLEGE WOULD DO THIS. ALSO, THIS SHOWS A LACK OF PLANNING AND MAY INDICATE A LACK OF DUE DILIGENCE.

A Second Corollary to the first one above is:

> NEVER ASSIGN YOUR OWN BOOK UNLESS YOU ALLOW STUDENTS TO OBTAIN IT AT BELOW COST AND YOU HAVE COMPLIED WITH ALL UNIVERSITY RULES. YOU SHOULD NEVER PROFIT FROM YOUR STUDENTS' PURCHASES OF YOUR BOOK. THIS IS UNCONSCIONABLE AND MAY POSE A VIOLATION OF THE LAW.

State Ethics Rules prohibit Professors from obtaining financial gain while employed full-time by the University. I don't think it is a good idea for a Professor to assign his/her book to the class he/she teaches. At UConn, only two of my professors did this. There were only two exceptions to my general rule. Let me explain these exceptions as clearly as I can from my perspective.

The University of Connecticut (when I attended) had a policy of inviting some famous people to Storrs to teach for usually a one-year appointment. While I was there, two prominent authors were invited. One was Samuel Lubell who authored "The Future of American Politics," and was an early pollster who knocked on doors to canvass voters. He was known for his ability to predict electoral outcomes. Well needless to say, Sam was hired to teach a class about his book, so obviously he would have had to assign his book. He did. If the University hires someone to teach the material one wrote and researched for the purpose of making it a class, then I would agree that one was hired for that very purpose and expected to assign one's book. In this case, the University tacitly approves of the use of the author's book. If any ethical issues exist, the issues are thereby waived. Sam's class was small and was held in the Political Science Conference room. His book was interesting and clearly not assigned to make him royalties. There were only five to ten people taking the class.

The second person invited to the school was the great Nigerian writer, Chinua Achebe. He was invited to teach a class in "African Literature". Mr. Achebe assigned his book, "Things Fall Apart," and I recall buying the book not really paying too much attention to the fact our instructor was the author. This was not the case for Lubell's class. I did not know whether this author was invited to specifically discuss his book(s).

It was 1975 through 1976. I did learn that Professor Achebe was being considered for the Nobel Prize for one of his books. I later learned that literary circles were writing Achebe should have been awarded the honor, but was disgustingly overlooked. After reading the book ("Things Fall Apart"), I learned a lot about African Literature from a different perspective. The basic lesson I learned was that Achebe's book was

57

instrumental in influencing most, if not all, African Writers post publication of his book in the 1960's. His book had a clear, direct effect on all those writers coming afterward.

I got to know this author personally. He was a gentle spoken and meek man. His writings influenced many peoples' perspective on Africa. The world only learned about Africa, prior to Achebe's writings, from a slanted British perspective. This one-sided approach often learned in history has been later determined to be biased and incorrect.

I gained tremendous insight into one man's approach - through literature, to change the world and its perspective. He changed the way people now viewed African History and Literature. It was hard to see how bias and prejudice affects perspective. We only know what we learn. Sometimes our learning is flawed by the way events are reported and taught. One-sided perspective is a one-way street. Multidimensional perspective is a two-way street.

As we read the follow up books assigned by Achebe and written by other African writers, I remember laughing and joking with him. I recall saying to him-"Why you son-of-a gun" when I finally understood what he had done. He sparked a type of enlightenment if you will. This man, through his writings, influenced the entire world -this meek, humble man. He contributed to a better understanding of his country, and a better respect for his fellow African authors. He ignited a flame. Anyhow, he walked over to me, smiled at me, and gave me a pat on the shoulder. He was saying in a unique professor's way, "a job well-done". I know he appreciated the fact that I had understood what he had accomplished through his writings. He did not assign his book to make a profit. He did so to help us understand his very special role and the contribution of his books. This is what he did. He changed the way America and the West and the World viewed his writings and his African colleagues' writings. His perspective was a new one. It was a hidden and true perspective. He was a tremendous writer who made a enormous impact. He made a difference. He made us realize that Africa and its people are not backward, ignorant, and uncivilized. He made us realize that Africans have their own culture. Further, he made us realize that African culture is just as rich, beautiful and civilized as our own culture. He made us realize that we can learn from this culture and assimilate the lessons taught into our own. He made us realize that we do not need to civilize these people. He made us realize that these people are civilized in ways we simply do not understand. He made us realize that if savagery truly exists, it exists simply in our failure to understand African culture. He made us realize that we needed to learn this. He made us realize that Ignorance is bliss for all countries.

I recall telling him, "you used your book to influence all of these other writers". When I said that, I realized that the other writers influenced were not just African writers. The writers influenced were world renown. He changed the world for the better. He educated us. As I think about this today, I marvel at this accomplishment.

He just meekly smiled. We both laughed out loud. I felt proud to be there and in this man's class. He was not a boisterous or a loud man. He was not a conceited man. He was simply a great man and a great writer. I never thought African Lit could influence me. It was related to my major as will be discussed later.

As I reminisce, I realize that this man left his mark by bringing about beneficial social change. He forced people to reexamine history written by outsiders tainted by their biases and prejudices. He influenced the world to reconsider errors clarified by his writings. I ask myself frankly how many professors assigning their own books have done so with such noble intentions? How many have done so to illustrate the need to spark immediate change under such circumstances? I think the point is well-taken.

When a teacher considers using his/her own book for class, I suggest a type of analysis should be taken. First, is there a real need to assign one's own book in the first place? Second, is there a better authority to use? Third, is there a protocol that must be followed prior to assignment of the book? I would suggest shying away from doing so. I would also suggest caution.

Of course, if the Professor's book is the ultimate authority used nationwide, I suppose First Amendment implications arise. Absent such compelling circumstances, I think discretion is the better part of valor.

Of course, if I write a book that is the actual subject of the class, like the example I used regarding Sam's book, it makes little sense not to use that book for the reasons already mentioned. In Sam's case, when he assigned his book "The Future of American Politics, it is interesting to note that he did not assign ten other books with it.

At Southern, if a Professor is planning to assign his/her book, the Administration has a protocol that must be met. The Professor should seek approval first. The protocol should always be used and strictly followed. The only exception to that protocol would be the unique situation which includes the professor's symbolic speech rights. If the book is the best authority in the field, or has influenced a whole new way of thinking, (like Mr. Achebe's books,) then I would argue that a Professor who assigns that type of book is constitutionally protected by his/her symbolic speech rights of the First Amendment. To be safe, I would simply abide by the protocol prior to jumping the gun. The ethics statutes should always be complied with first. In this way, the Professor is complying with the University protocol and thereby safe in that regard.

Connecticut State Ethics Statutes protect both Professors and the University from conflicts of interest. For example, a professor should not make a financial gain on his/her students. Profits from selling texts to students fall squarely within that prohibition. If a professor assigns his/her book at cost, with no profit to the professor, then there is no violation of the ethical rules. If a professor gives the book away, that too would be fine.

Professors have access to student confidential information. If a Professor improperly views and/or dispenses confidential information, he/she will also run afoul of the state ethics prohibitions. Of course, sexual relationships between students and teachers are prohibited. These are but a few examples of the provisions we need to know and respect. I suppose a teacher could always make his/her book optional, and place it on reserve for any of the students to view at no cost to them. In any event, Chinua Achebe's book is the exception to the rule for the reasons given.

In 1976, I had the pleasure of studying American-International Relations with Dr.

John Plank. John was an adviser to the Kennedy Administration on US-Cuba Relations, and was known for sending a telegram to the President warning him against the Bay of Pigs Invasion. Plank stated in that telegram that any effort to overthrow Castro would be futile. Dr. Plank was a brilliant teacher. He was a perfectionist. He was a skinny man with a well-trimmed thin mustache. He was a pleasant Professor who enjoyed his classes and students. He was entertaining, witty, funny and down to earth.

I liked Professor Plank and wanted to do well in his class. He generated a warmth for teaching and learning. He was always punctual, prepared, and motivated. Everyone liked him and enjoyed his class. He made learning fun and was always attentive to the student's questions and concerns. He was very knowledgeable. If asked a question, he answered calmly, clearly and correctly.

My only gripe was that when I completed all the course work, I had received an average of 89.6. I thought to myself that it was my very best. I was proud I did well because most of my classmates stated Plank was a tough grader. Well, he really was. I thought with class participation, I would surely receive an A-. Needless to say, that did not happen. I received a B+. I was not a happy camper when I received my grade. Although I was disappointed, I never held a grudge against Dr. Plank. I still respected him, and came to understand that it was simply the way he chose to effectively grade his students. He was firm but fair. He gave me what I earned. There was no mistake. I received what I deserved, and that was the end of it.

I told myself that if I were ever to teach a class, and if a student of mine received an

89.5 and was a participant in class, that I would most assuredly give that student an A or A- based upon his or her participation. I guess this was my way of rebelling against the harsh grading policy I experienced at UConn. Was this a curse or a blessing? THIS WAS LESSON FIVE.

I also had Professor Max Thatcher for American Political Ideology. Max was an older gentleman who was truly funny. He dedicated himself to his students and was big on attendance. He expected you to be there. He was witty, polite, and loved telling jokes in class. Everyone felt welcome and hated missing class. He learned everyone's name very quickly in the semester and would call on the student by name. Max's door was always open for his or any student wishing to stop in. Although he was getting up there in age, I realized that Max's students identified with him as a role model. They loved him and respected him. He was a dedicated professional trying to help his students in any way he could. I told myself that if I were ever to teach a class, I would try to be there for my students like Max was there for me. I did not want to be someone who simply went through the motions. I wanted to be someone who was like Max. Max went above and beyond the call of duty for his students.

My reason was clear. Dedicated and unique teachers like Max were truly gifts from God. They shine a ray of hope on their students. I never forgot that about Max. Teachers are hired for the students. The teacher's role often makes a difference. Dr. Rai would always tell me that and would also say without the students, there is no need for (us) teachers. Teachers affect all professions. They are like catalysts affecting their students in beneficial ways. Their contributions are enormous. I learned from Max that good teachers are role models. The students recognize the good teachers and always maintain that recognition throughout their entire lives. THIS WAS LESSON SIX.

As I write this, I learned that Dr. I. Ridgeway Davis, another professor I had just passed away. I took Dr. Davis for Law and the Political Community in 1976. This class is comparable to the class I teach at Southern called United States Legal Systems. Dr. Davis was a slender man who I got to know quite well. I recall one class whereby he was trying to explain the difference between legal and equitable remedies. He would call the legal remedies, "liggel" and I would laugh whenever I heard him say liggel. I recall meeting with him on several occasions to discuss Alexander Bickel's book "The Least Dangerous Branch." We would argue over the role of the Court in society. We both agreed with one thing: Alex was brilliant. I specifically recall one of our conversations. I told Dr. Davis that I recall the last time I heard Alex speak. It was on the radio in early August of 1974, while he was being interviewed regarding Sam Ervin's Watergate Investigation. Bickel was asked what he thought of the Watergate Committee Hearings. I was in the car when the question came over the radio. I remember stopping the car so I could listen to the interview. Bickel stated and I quote: "These Watergate Hearings are the beginning of the end of the Nixon Administration". I told Dr. Davis how I knew Alex was very sick when he gave that phone interview. He was suffering from cancer and a brain tumor if my current recollection is correct and did not live much longer after that interview. In any event, we then discussed how Nixon resigned shortly after hearing Bickel's comments. I made it clear to Dr. Davis that when Nixon

64

announced his resignation, I specifically recall the President stating that it (his resignation) was to become effective noon the next day (August 9th, 1974). Professor Davis said, "I wonder why he waited until noon"? I recall telling Davis that I believe it was due to Nixon's promise he made to nominate Thomas Meskill to the Second Circuit Court of Appeals. Dr. Davis stated that he understood that President Ford nominated Meskill to the Bench. (I believe Davis thought I was blowing smoke somewhere.) I replied, "yes, but Nixon kept his word and started the paperwork for Ford". I told Dr. Davis that I was of the opinion that Nixon kept his word and made sure that the new President (Ford) followed through before his resignation became effective. I will never forget the smile on his face. It lit-up the entire room. I just did not think Dr. Davis believed me. I also recall telling Dr. Davis that I thought Alexander Bickel, had he lived, would have been nominated and confirmed to take Justice William O. Douglas' place. I stated that this would surely be the most logical choice, since both men were known for their Yale affiliation. Both were "hot shot" Yale Law Professors. Dr. Davis got a kick out of my comment "hot shot" and smiled at me. He enjoyed our conversation.

Dr. Davis will be remembered for his dedication to his students. He was always kind and he will be sorely missed. He left his mark on UConn, his students, and his Department. Ridgeway was instrumental in preparing his many students for thousands or more legal careers. He was a legend at UConn.

As I think of Dr. Davis, I smile. My class included many students who went on to become attorneys. I was one. Bill Lipman was another. Bill went on to become a Part A Criminal Clerk in New Haven. Bill and I would talk about those days and recall

Dr. Davis and the UConn Political Science Department. Dr. Davis' impact cannot be ignored; he had a profound effect on all of us. He made his mark then as we make our mark now. He has permitted us to pass it on. Great teachers have a way of doing this- simply of making us better. We become better people, better teachers, and better professionals. Guys like Professor Davis have such an impact. We continue to feel that impact even as time goes by.

Just as an aside, I remember Davis' secretary who was named Cheryl. I would kid her and request that she straighten Professor Davis out regarding his pronunciation of the word legal. She never bit. She would say "Why don't you tell him"? We both laughed. Yes, I guess that was surely not going to happen anytime soon. Those are "liggel remedies" that I will never forget. He never said legal. He always said liggel. With all fun aside, the man knew his stuff. His dedication and hard work at UConn were monumental. If anyone could say liggel, and have the perfect right to do so, Ridgeway Davis was that person. He earned the right to say it any way he wanted. He was a legal scholar among us. It was an honor to have him in class. My greatest tribute to him is the fact that my class, United States Legal Systems, mirrors his. (What an honor to say that!). Yes, my class in many ways is the mirror image of his class. There is simply no better way to honor a person. His impact on me in many ways is my impact on them.

Last but not least, I would like to mention Dr. Louis Gerson once again. I took Lou's class on U.S. Foreign Policy. Lou was a big man. He always wore his hair long. When I would see him walking around campus, he usually would have his head down (and had a lot on his mind). That observation was very clear and not an exaggeration. When I would see him, I would always go over to him to say hi to Lou. I would always tell him to "Smile, Dr. Gerson", and he would stop, perk up, smile, and waive. I wanted to take him away from that pensive loneliness which appeared to be his own dark edge of the world. It appeared to me to be a dark place. It bothered me. Lou was a wonderful man. He was always pleasant as my mentor and I studied hard with him taking an independent course requirement for my "Honor's Thesis". Lou's eagerness together with his motivational approach enlightened me like no other teacher. He was brilliant.

I recall speaking to Dr. Walsh about Lou. David told me that Lou and his mother were fortunate enough to leave Poland in 1938 prior to the Nazi Occupation. Gerson and his mother just escaped in the nick of time. Many of Lou's family members who remained were later victims of the Nazi Occupation and were killed. I never knew that.

Lou was a tough person to describe. He was a hard worker and expected others to work hard. Although his uniqueness is hard to explain, I will try my best to describe Lou by way of events and circumstances I witnessed firsthand.

Due to the massive respect I had for Lou, I made sure I was always prepared and on time. I truly admired him and considered myself fortunate to be able to study with him. He was a talented man. We both agreed that I would do my thesis on his specialty of American Foreign Policy. He knew I wanted to go to law school, so Lou had me focus my research on clear legal issues. He helped me narrow those issues for purposes of doing my research and writing. (He wanted some aspect of law to come into this.)

Lou suggested I read Henry Kissinger's thesis written while he was at Harvard: "A

World Restored". Kissinger analyzed some of the errors made by World Leaders in the early eighteenth and nineteenth centuries and derived a list of do's and don'ts for future diplomats and foreign policy experts. The book was a pragmatic approach used to teach some important points learned from clear historical blunders. Lou used the book to explain a few points to me that I often think about today. Remember, I took Lou over forty-two years ago. His instruction then still has an important impact on me today. For example, Lou's instruction clearly brought concepts together for me while simultaneously explaining the relevance of all this to the teaching profession. I will try to explain how Lou was able to inspire me the way he did. It is magic. It reminds me of those few instances in life we all experience that are quite unique and are hard to replicate. I will try to explain it and hope I will do justice to it.

Dr. Gerson had the most direct impact on me while I was at UConn. He was the guy. To this day, I must say, I never had anyone whose influence comes close to that of Lou's. I cannot stress that point enough. He was truly the man who brought it all together for me. Explanation of all this is hard to mention and difficult to articulate.

Lou always explained that any professor worth his/her (salt) position must have a mastery of the subject area he/she teaches. Areas where one is not experienced should not be areas assigned (to or taught by) that professor. He would say that common sense dictates that one knows his/her competency levels. People experienced in drama should not necessarily be teaching classes in rocket science. This sounds simple. The same rule applies to our Political Science Professors. Just because someone is a member of a

68

Department does not mean that he/she can teach all of the subject areas. Schools that permit this to happen should not be allowed to do this. This is almost like taking a fish out of water and expecting the fish to walk. This is a terrible harm sometimes practiced on students. No Department Chair should permit this to occur. We all should know our competency levels. We have an obligation to our Department and our School not to perform this type of fraud on our students. It is tantamount to stealing a student's right to a competent instructor in a particular subject area. Further, this action harms the reputation of the school. I remember laughing when Lou stated to me that if the teacher does not know his/her competency levels, then we are all in trouble. Some Professors do take on courses they simply should not agree to teach. I made it a point to never agree to teach a class I am not competent to teach. Lou made it a point to stress this to me. It rings loud and clear even today. Evidently, some teachers fall into that pit.

I then got lost and did not comprehend what Dr. Gerson continued to say. When I was not clear I would ask Dr. Gerson to try to repeat and to explain himself, thinking to myself that I really did not want to leave Lou with the impression that I was not paying attention, or worst, that I was simply stupid. After all, I noticed we were going off on a tangent, and I was getting left far behind. I did not like that feeling when I was with Lou.

He took a moment to explain in detail what his thoughts were. I remember this communication as if it occurred yesterday and I have visualized Lou telling me this time and time again. His comments went something like this and note that I can only paraphrase. The gist of the communication went something like this:

Frank, a professor must understand his subject-matter
very well. He/she must be able to analyze situations
in a way that is useful to others. We, as professors
(meaning Henry Kissinger and his Department Colleagues),
must be able to rise above the subject-matter in such a way as to
contribute to society in a meaningful way. We do not write
for the mere sake of writing(publishing), but we write to share
our ideas with others. We write to educate. We write to help
others, including politicians, to understand. We write to better
society of its ills, and to not perpetrate those ills, but
to identify, isolate, and to eradicate them. This is what we are
here to do. We must make a difference. We do this to better
ourselves, our students, our departments, and our (schools)
Universities. This is "our mission". It is an awesome responsibility. Try not to forget what I am telling you. It is
very important. We are here to contribute and are here for
that reason. Professors don't just teach. To be effective, we
must be more than just teachers. We must bring about change
for the better through teaching our students.

As I recall, I do not know why and how he and I got off on this tangent. Maybe it had

something to do with the fact that often times people view professors as living off of the

largess? You know, I think Lou was upset with the way some people portray University

Professors as lazy, useless and a "dime a dozen". Maybe it was an impression he got

from reading an article that day, who knows? I see it today with the mentality

surrounding State givebacks.

I was glad to have Dr. Gerson. This man was not just an intellectual; he truly

understood the benefit of education in practical terms. He used Henry Kissinger's model/

thesis to illustrate this point. He understood the true mission of the University. Although

we are individuals, and often go it alone, when we act in our professional capacity we

rise above who we are to do the right thing and to help others. We must try our hardest

to always contribute our talents to society. This also applies to political affiliation. We,

70

as professionals, rise above politics. I guess I saw this when Kissinger was recently asked if he would help President Trump. Kissinger stated helping our President is what we must do and is above politics. It is our role to help the President any way we can. This is what we do. Politics is not an issue. We give up our personal idiosyncrasies. We all hope he (the President) will do well and we will help him in any way we can. We go beyond ourselves to help others. (This was the point Dr. Gerson was trying to make.)

We do this through long hours of research. We do this through long hours of arduous analysis. We do this through long hours of teaching. We do this through dedicating our lives to education. The end result is to make people, our schools, and our government better. It is never a selfish endeavor. We give ourselves for the benefit of others.

In this way we too are students. Learning is this dynamic process (I mentioned earlier). It was something like I learned from Chinua Achebe. It is not short-sighted or myopic. It was as if the two men were brothers. In many ways they truly were. I felt so small, almost like a baby learning to crawl, truly not comprehending any of this until Gerson and Achebe taught it to me. I learned it from them. I luckily did not miss the boat. I got it, damn it, and thank God, I did. This was something worthwhile. It was life-aspiring. It reiterated the fact that "Education" is a dynamic process. It is a process that needs thinking and rethinking based upon newer and better research. With new research we learn a better understanding of things past, present and future. Education is a tool and must always be multifaceted on so many levels. There often is not a simple way, or the best way to proceed. As long as one learns and one keeps an open mind while learning, one will keep the process active, alive, and dynamic. Once you or anyone else for that matter, becomes too comfortable, it is time to rethink and regroup and re-plan. There is no room for complacency in learning. The process is ever expanding, like the Universe in order to fulfill its vital mission.

The world keeps changing and the moving parts always need to be reviewed and reexamined. It is almost like greasing the wheels. We have to keep checking and maintaining ourselves. The correct answer today may be the incorrect answer tomorrow. How can that be? Learning and Education are so complex. Our roles are often complex.

It is more than learning for the sake of learning. We don't study for the mere purpose of learning. We do more than that. We effectively learn to contribute to society. We must often put our own special effort or touch on it. We must make it our own. We must create. Teaching is the art of creating new and better ways to learn. It is symbiotic.

For example, if I teach United States Government, I must see the relevant issues and problems and I must be able to research the issues with an eye to synthesizing a resolution or solution. There is no vacuum. Our students and society look to us for guidance. That is a pretty awesome responsibility. Teachers are similar to lawyers, in that they are problem solvers- plain and simple. How do we competently educate our students so they can reach their life-aspiring goals? This is like a mother/father helping his/her son/daughter to walk. We teach in a similar way. Our efforts must make a difference. We are vital forces procuring beneficial social change. We are engineers who create beneficial and positive social change. Dr. Gerson made me realize this. I never understood that part of education or of the role teachers' play. It was truly a rewarding afternoon discussing all of this with Dr. Gerson. I never forgot his words. He simply taught me much more than the course material. I guess I finally understood the meaning of dedication. I finally understood how and why great teachers, like Lou Gerson, tended to make a difference. Great teachers simply tend to do this. They inspire. They cultivate. They help us comprehend things. He did this for me. He really helped me. He was there for me. He made me understand clearly and competently. He encouraged and enlightened me. Lou lit the candle for me. It was almost like the spark Achebe lit. A spark ignited into a conflagration. The true value of education cannot be underestimated. I did not truly understand him until I thought hard about all of Lou's comments. I marvel at the thought: How can a teacher have such an impact on a student?

When I taught, I always tried to put Lou's words to work. I always tried to examine and reexamine things along the guidelines he set. In preparation for class, I would always outline my thoughts and ideas. There was simply no room in my classroom for static rote teaching or rote learning. It was dynamics preparation and dynamic classroom discussion. The process got better with time. It was adaptive. I was adaptive. My students were adaptive. This was a good approach that worked well. I had to make it better. I always analyzed and reviewed my assignments to make the class presentation better than the one before. I always contemplated ways to improve it.

Before I go on, understand that this is what I learned from Lou, and is not meant to criticize any approach used by others. As Lou stated often, education and learning are multifaceted, and there are really many different approaches that can be used which will work. The approaches used can and will vary based up the class, level (undergraduate or graduate), the students (all freshman versus most if not all seniors or upperclassman), etc. I suppose the initial question is whether my approach (used) reflects the static approach or the dynamic approach. This question is relatively simple and to lie to myself purposely makes me play a fool's errand. We simply cannot fool ourselves. When we teach a class for a long time, we tend to fit into the mold of comfort directing us to the static approach. We may start off as dynamic but evolve to static. We always need to be wary of this trap and to guard against it at all cost. This is not good.

If President Donald Trump is thinking about using his Pardon Power on himself, or his family members, most people might say, "well, he is the President and he has the Power, so why not?" A lawyer would look at that action as an 'abuse of the President's Official Authority' subjecting him to Impeachment by Congress. A Political Science Professor may look at the gridlock in Congress and determine that the split along party lines will not permit a successful impeachment. I suppose the point here is that teachers who view the issue realize the solution created by our Founders cannot work due simple gridlock. Do we stop there? Do we think of ways to effectively deal with the issue? Surely most people grasp the problem. If we recognize that the problem cannot be solved by the current political atmosphere, then we must analyze all of the options or an amendment process. Gridlock is nothing new. A different approach is due. If you don't have any idea or clue whatsoever, then you should work to find one. As some of my colleagues would say, perhaps there is the need for a constitutional amendment to deal with grid-lock when Congress cannot act. It could take the form of an amendment

74

allowing a national referendum placing the issue squarely on the ballot for the American People to decide. Let the people break the gridlock. Maybe the answer should include more democracy and not less. Professors should research and articulate policy positions to resolve everyday conflicts they are skilled to address. THIS WAS LESSON SEVEN.

I know I have been saying this time and time again. If you teach U.S. Government, it is simply not enough to comprehend the various issues and address them in class. It is vital to discuss these issues and to try to address them in such a way as to construct a reasonably articulate plan in class for problem solving resolutions. It is simply not enough to say this is the issue and problem, so let Congress deal with it. An analysis of the issues in an attempt to stimulate thought towards a resolution is the key to synthesis. Once an answer is synthesized, the next step must be action even if just to contact our politicians. We must always remember that the most important theme in United States Government classes is one that emphasizes that "Good Citizens" must always get involved. If we see a problem and know that it exists, we should never turn our back on that problem. If we do, then we deserve what we get. Educated professionals have a higher duty in this regard. Inaction on our part is simply unthinkable. We must practice what we preach in class. If we do not practice what we preach, we are hypocrites. The example we are supposed to set for our students is lost. We cease to be role models.

I suppose that hindsight is always twenty-twenty. After the 2000 election when Gore won the popular vote and Bush won the electoral vote, Hillary Clinton proposed doing

75

away with the Electoral College. We know that did not happen. Could you imagine (Let's pretend for a moment), had Hillary been instrumental in proposing a constitutional amendment to do so and had it passed, she would have been our President in the 2016 election. This is what I mean by doing more than just speaking about changing the Electoral College or teaching and preaching about it. Hillary clearly identified the problem. Most Americans recognized it and simply shrugged the problem away. We all knew about the problem. Unfortunately, no action was taken to remedy the problem. It is also interesting to note that even after the 2016 election, we still do not hear much about any legislative attempts to correct the process. I wonder why? Could it be because President Trump believes he won the popular vote? (but for, electoral fraud?). I suppose we cannot and should not ignore the "great historical significance" of the Electoral College. This point alone makes Congress skeptical to eradicate it. If we could propose an Amendment that does not do that, but possibly allows for the popular vote to govern in uniquely close races, we could split the baby whereby we have our cake and eat it too. Basically, we could look at history and provide for contingencies should this or that occur. We could allow it to work when it does work, but allow for exceptions when the process calls for it. (Specifically, when one candidate wins the popular vote and the other the electoral vote - this should be clearly an indication that the exception, (whatever the amendment provides), should govern.

Divided Government means paralysis. We may see this better should Congress issue Articles of Impeachment today, with insufficient support to prevail. Does all this ring a bell? I suppose the Founders only expected an Impeachment of a sitting President to succeed in times of grave misconduct rising to the level of "high crimes and misdemeanors". Abuse of one's official conduct could also mean "obstruction of justice", "conspiracy to obstruct justice", "severe conflict of interest", etc. These issues bring about memories of the Nixon and Clinton Administrations.

The issues mentioned cannot excuse Professors from the task before them to research and resolve these complex sociopolitical problems. After all, this is a role we play in society. Yes, we teach our students, but we also teach our politicians and citizens how our remarkable Government works so well. This is our unique role. Do we perform with flying colors, or do we ignore our role? This is precisely what we do. This is our vital societal function. After all, not everyone, can be a Professor of Political Science. We write and publish ideas to resolve serious societal issues. That is simply our function. We do it well, or we never stop trying to do it well. We never give up.

I would have to meet with Dr. Gerson once to twice a week. I got to know his secretary Florence quite well. She too was at Dr. Gerson's memorial service. She recognized me, and said, "well, you are at least one person I recognize". I gave her a big hug and kiss. I remembered how I would stop by the political science office to see Lou, and how she would always say, "you know, he's awfully busy and you really shouldn't just stop by without an appointment". I would ask if I could wait to see if he could fit me in, and Lou would never let me down; He would say "Frank, come-on in". I would then look at Florence and see the frustration on her face and just smile as Lou and I would enter his office. I felt like the cat that ate the canary when that happened. I reminded her of this and she remembered how gracious Lou was. He would never turn a student away. At least, he never turned me away. I can surely say this from first hand experience. In fact, Dr. David Walsh, my colleague at Southern was writing his PH. D. with Lou back then. When I would arrive to see Lou, Dave would usually be at the office first waiting to see him. Lou would always take me first despite David being there ahead of me. Years later, David and I would reminisce about those college days back in the 1970's. I recall David asking me why I was there waiting to see Gerson. You see, Lou was head of the Department and had a very limited teaching schedule because he was also assigned other important administrative functions. I told Dave why I was there, and he simply smiled. We were both fortunate to have crossed paths with Dr. Gerson. I mention this personal touch Lou had with us and other students I am sure.

When I later was hired at Southern, David remembered me. We both recognized each other from our UConn days. When Dave and I attended the memorial service for Lou, we realized that one thing was certain: Great Professors are sorely missed but never truly forgotten. Their impact on us remain with us forever. There can be no greater tribute to a teacher than that simple statement. We both agreed. That awesome responsibility I spoke about earlier did not go unrecognized or unfulfilled. Lou fulfilled his responsibility with us and we in turn fulfilled our responsibility with our students.

Lou was unique in class. He had written on U.S. Foreign Policy and was known for his biography of John Foster Dulles. Despite his accomplishments, Lou was always approachable and kind. He motivated his students by captivating their interests. In fact, he would always speak well of other professors he knew. One of those people he praised in my class was Dr. John Iatrides, a Southern Professor who I later met as one of my colleagues. I was so proud to tell John about Lou's praise. Both John and Lou were always kind and dedicated and cut from the same mold. I remember Lou best by the way he ran the Political Science Department. Lou, like Dr. Rai, felt that the teachers have an awesome responsibility to their students, and in fact were there primarily for the students. He always tried to act in the best interests of his students. He always took pride in his students and their accomplishments. Lou, like Kul were unique men. Both were unique and their legacy lives on.

I recall one appointment with Lou in particular. Gerson was opening up his mail, and appeared quite annoyed when I arrived. I said, "Dr. Gerson, what's the matter"? "Am I taking too much of your time"? He looked up at me and said "Frank, no, I just got the tuition bills for my kids". "One is at Yale, and the other is at Harvard". "They're breaking me". I smiled and said, " how come they don't go here"? Lou looked at me right in the eye and said, "that would be too easy". We both laughed for a moment and then got off to work on my thesis. I always felt a personal connection with him. He was a gem of a guy.

I knew tuition was steep at Yale because I had applied there. I believe at the time it was close to $20,000 but am not all that sure. UConn was substantially less; I recall living on campus in the mid 1970's was approximately $2,200 a semester or about $5,000 a year. It probably was a bit less. In any event, I cannot be sure but think Lou probably would have received a tuition break had he sent his children to UConn. What an irony? Of course, that is usually how things work out. I decided that if I were ever to teach a class I would make sure my kids go to the school if eligible for tuition reimbursement. In fact, this did occur when my daughter graduated from high school; although Annie did quite well on her PSAT and SAT's, she chose to attend Southern and was fortunate enough to qualify for tuition reimbursement or a tuition waiver while I continued to teach. This was something I learned from Lou. Why go elsewhere, when you can go here? I know Lou would have agreed with me. I often wondered why his children did not attend UConn. I know Yale is a great school, but so is UConn. Yale, for all its greatness did not have Dr. Louis Gerson as head of its Political Science Department. THIS WAS LESSON EIGHT.

In any event, I said to myself, if I were ever to teach a class, I would like to be a member of University Department similar to the one Lou ran. I would want to be a member of a department that treats everyone with respect and dignity. I would like to be a member of a department that treats everyone like a family. That was the way Lou ran his department. Everyone was kind and respectful. No one ever spoke poorly of anyone else. This was true of all members of the department. The department included all staff, especially the secretary with all others working together harmoniously to make the University a great place to learn. At the memorial service, Florence told me she was hurt because the Political Science Department failed to inform her about Lou's service. She stated she was informed second-hand. I emailed the UConn Department Head, Prof. David Yalof, to let him know what Florence said. He responded by stating that everyone received email notice. I explained to him that sometimes email is simply not good enough when messaging older people like myself and Florence. This was one of those situations that required more, if you know what I mean. I explained how Lou admired Florence, as we all did. I mentioned that this was not the Political Science Department that I remembered. This statement made me recall a recent occurrence.

As Jean, our long-time secretary mentioned to me at my retirement party, " Frank", she said, "once you are a member of this Department, you have to die to leave". Boy did that make me feel good. Jean always had a way of doing that-making (us) the members of our department feel better despite having a bad day. I believe that sentiment basically says it all. Your Department is the heart of your mission. Your colleagues are the blood that keeps the mission going. It is your family. I learned this vital lesson from Lou and Florence. I suppose no one likes to be left out once having been a part of the mission. We are all in it until "death do us part". THIS WAS LESSON NINE.

I mention these few moments to illustrate how we are influenced by others. There is no doubt that my undergraduate professors had more influence on me than my law school professors. Unfortunately, none of my law professors had the impact that Dr. Gerson had on me. In any event, I came away from my undergraduate studies with a firm commitment to higher education. I learned something I never realized; I learned how important education is to succeed in life. This was clear to me by the impact it had(s) on me. The key to success is education. I was once told by the late President Gerald Ford that "time and perseverance are the keys to success". He was referring to my application to Yale. I changed my mind and attended UConn anyhow thanking him for his advice. As I think back, Yale had Joe LaPalombara in its Political Science Department, but UConn had Lou Gerson in its Political Science Department. There is no doubt that I made the right decision. Joe was super, but Lou was superb.

So, teaching played a big part in my life. I always tried to consider how I could make a difference. Making a difference meant trying harder to help others. Our success is measured by the beneficial impact our efforts have on others. I thought one way to benefit people is through the practice of law. That is also correct. Teaching is another way to bring about beneficial social change. I did learn, though, that without my legal education, I probably would not have become a teacher. I suppose the study of law does have its benefits. Judge William Holden told me this. The law has, at the very least, allowed me the opportunity. It has opened the door. It has allowed me to gain tremendous experience in the state, federal and tax courts which has in turn allowed me to share with my students. My work experience in my field of study has helped me enrich my classes. I guess that is a lesson worthy of mentioning. THIS WAS A LESSON TEN.

Chapter Five: 1986:
THE EARLIER TEACHING YEARS

I began teaching at Southern in the fall of 1986. I sent a resume in to the Political Science Department and was contacted in August by the Department's secretary, Jean. I guess there was a last-minute cancellation by someone, and Jean was given the authority to hire someone. It was a lucky day for me. I was asked if I would be interested in teaching United States Government, and I said that I would be happy to instruct this class.

Jean helped me with all the paperwork and gave me the run down. Jean was then and is still now, a no-nonsense-type. I knew the second I met her that she was a vital part of the Department. I simply mean she ran the entire department all by herself-literally.

She made sure everyone got their syllabus in, and she made sure everything ran calmly and efficiently. Slowly but surely, she introduced me to everyone. Jean instructed me on Departmental protocol. For example, you must prepare a syllabus and make sure that she has a copy for the Department records. I was told to always be on time, and that our Department prides itself on following University Rules and Policy. We run a tight ship here and our Department is a model Department at Southern. It was like boot camp without the camp, but with a well-trained sergeant. Boy was she tough. In terms of butting heads with someone, kindly give me the sergeant over Jean any time.

I never once had a problem with Jean. She was articulate, clever, witty, and reminded me a lot of Florence who was not as assertive as Jean was, but surely just as nice. We all loved the way she managed the Department. I never met anyone more efficient. It was a tightly run ship in all kinds of waters-turbulent or calm.

What do I recall about my first few classes? I recall having the United States Government text chosen by another Professor. After all, I was hired late and there was simply no time to change the original teacher's choice. I did not like the text because it reminded me of a comic book. I remember saying to myself "gee, this is college". Any way, I made it work but made sure that I did not have to use that particular text any longer if I continued to teach at Southern.

This particular incident brought to mind the situation with Henry at UConn. I finally understood that sometimes book choice is not the error of the teacher. Sometimes the teacher simply inherits the text. Well, I was definitely a step-child in that regard.

I recall that my first classes were quite large. I recall lecturing about federalism, and giving the class a hypothetical about a fictitious state legalizing marijuana for medicinal and recreational purposes based upon its own state constitutional protections. One student got upset because he was in law enforcement and felt that the hypo undermined his duties (the war on drugs was a big thing back then). Surely, I never intended to offend anyone and I learned to be careful about offending students. This was not a good thing to do in any class but does unfortunately happen.

I also recall telling my students that if they participated in class, that I reserved the right to raise their grades one-third. I would always document this in the syllabus stating exactly how many assignments would be graded and how I would calculate the grades. I would also clearly explain the point allotment and the percentages each test/paper would have on their final grades. I always made this crystal clear to my students.

Unfortunately, the statement about reserving the right to raise one's grade did cause an issue. One young lady actually received an A- for the course, but only after I had raised her grade from a B+ because of credit she received for class participation. The student became upset when she learned what her final grade would be and made an appointment with me to go over her exam in detail. The student came in and very angrily demanded an "A". I tried to explain to her that I had already raised her grade, but she was furious none-the-less. She kept telling me to simply give her a few more points and that would do it.

When she came to discuss her grade, Jean reminded me not to shut the door while I spoke with the student alone. This was something I did not realize. If I were in the room with the door closed, I could be setting myself up for all kinds of problems. I always re-member that first lesson I learned from Jean. Simply I should never make an unpleasant situation worse. Further, I should never bite off (open the door) to more than I could chew.

I took Jean's advice and left the office door wide-open. The student stated that she felt I should have given her an A. She stated that if I would just give her another few points once again that (that) would bring her to an A. I explained I had already raised her grade a third and if I raised her grade to an "A", I would then have to raise all the other students' grades. I tried to explain that I could not in good conscience just give her three or more points or any more points for that matter. This would give her an unfair advantage over other students, and simply was not permissible and was not going to happen. The student became very upset and stormed out of the office. I recall receiving a nasty note from this student a few years later. I immediately thought back to Dr. John Plank and now realized that maybe his approach of simply giving the student what he/she earned might in fact be the best policy. I now wondered whether Dr. Plank's approach was less fair or in reality better. I guess "you're damned if you do, and damned if you don't". I learned after my first year of teaching that it was not as easy as it looks. People who do not teach think the job is a breeze. It is like everything else in life in that it looks easier than it is. I suppose the grass is always greener somewhere else. Well, that supposition is incorrect. The task of trying to be fair to everyone is a full time job and is hard work.

Sometimes you simply have to be firm but fair. I learned that in Corrections when I was a correctional officer. You cannot favor anyone and simply must be fair with everyone. If you are firm but fair, you won't always be popular, but you will always be respected. One thing was certain, you only back down when you are wrong. I was not wrong, despite the fact I felt terrible about this incident and learned from it. This situation made me awfully careful when raising a student's grade. This made me clarify objective factors which supported my decision. I never wanted to be challenged on this again, and from that one time over thirty years ago, it truly never happened again. The only exception was one time when I simply made a computational error. You know, add- ing one and one and getting three. When a computational error is made, the teacher must always correct it. There is no discussion. It is the right thing to do making sure an apology is also forthcoming. A teacher's error must be acknowledged and always corrected. That is a given fact. (I wonder if this applies to prosecutors.)

The next thing I recall about the eighties was the affect the Reagan Administration had on my students. I mentioned this and think of the end of the Cold War. Many of my students for the first time were identifying with politics and politicians. Since the President was clearly a subject discussed by everyone, many of my students clearly identified with Ronald Reagan as the model political figure. President Ronald Reagan was a Republican. He was older and despite being in good shape, Reagan projected a Grandfather image to the students. Unlike my political identification with John F. Kennedy during the early sixties, I realized that the political socialization process encouraged many of the students to identify with Ronald Reagan as that ideal political candidate. He was the most visible to them. For my time, I saw Kennedy as that person because he was young when most of the world leaders were old and decrepit (Nikita Khruschchev, Moa Tse Tung, Josip Broz Tito, Charlesde-Gaulle, Franciso Franco). Kennedy represented youth and vitality.

Reagan was known as the "Great Communicator". He was the first actor elected President. I would explain in class that this fact meant that "Hollywood" was quite proud. I also stressed how Reagan did have political experience as Governor of the State of California. I tried to emphasize firsts. (Possible first actor, etc.). Reagan was a Republican who would compliment the Democrats for putting party affiliation aside to simply get things done in Congress. It was funny, one student remarked, "yep, when President Reagan got elected, I remember the TV stations playing 'Bed Time for Bonzo'

87

that whole week". I was fortunate enough to have an older student in class who remembered that fact. I said, "see, I told you Hollywood was impressed". During the last years of the eighties, students seemed very much concerned with simply getting through school as quickly as possible. This notion of graduating as quickly as possible does not seem to be the case today. I learned that the President is truly the most influential person in the U.S. Government course. This is partly due to his visibility. The President is seen everywhere (on television, on radio, in papers).

Recently with the Trump Administration, it is clear that a day does not pass without some type of intelligent discussion about the President in these classes. In the earlier days, the President was simply not as controversial as he is seen today. I say this in terms of the constant controversies we see with the New Administration. Some exceptions do exist for events or investigations like Watergate. With the Trump Administration, there appear to be Sexual Scandals, Russia Probes, White House Retention Issues, Immigration Enforcement Issues to simply name some of them. I cannot recall the start of any other Presidential Administration being as shaky and as controversial as compared with (to) the start of the Trump Administration today. I suppose I could be wrong but simply do not think I am wrong.

I must move forward with the Trump Administration. How do you teach this class today? We have a President who is very controversial. We have the most division I have seen in years. The best approach would simply to be objective, and allow the students to make their own determinations. Do we side with Government shutdown if Congress does not appropriate funds for "the wall?" (Lord help us.) Is this what politics is all about? Do we allow all illegal immigrants to be deported, when the prior Administration seems to have permitted a quicker and easier way to legal status for dreamers? Do we allow non-criminal illegals to go prior to deporting criminal illegals? Does it make a difference when we apply a blanket policy to all? What are the legal ramifications? Do we throw Obama Care out without having a replacement? Should ethics apply to the White House Staff and the President of the United States? Does the President have to be honest with the American People? Can a President be Impeached for lying to the American People? Can he be impeached for lying to the American people? Can Impeachment occur when divided government exists? If not, should Politics guarantee Presidential Immunity despite "high crimes and misdemeanors"? I suppose these questions are simple tests. These mentioned questions test our Government, our People, and our very lives. Should the Electoral College be amended or replaced? Asking questions is simply not enough. The American People deserve more. They deserve action. What is the course of that action? How do we proceed? Do we proceed?

Comparing Reagan to Trump is a great essay question. The role of the teacher in this environment is definitely an important one. The President is the product of his time and environment. Great Presidents have been able to survive the environments they are unfortunately placed in. Some were/are survivors, and others were/are not as fortunate. For example, we witnessed President Bush and 9/11; we witnessed Lincoln and the Civil War; we witnessed Nixon and Watergate. What will happen when President Trump is forced into a situation beyond his control. His actions and reactions will be historically significant to illustrate how well the political theorists will judge him. How well does Trump fit into a mold (pertaining to) or a theory of Presidential Character? Will he tarnish the White House, polish the White House, or simply have no effect at all on the White House. Some argue that question is moot.

In 1972, Professor James David Barber published his book "The Presidential Character: Predicting Performance in the White House. I believe Barber updated his book in 1977, and once in the mid 1980's and once again in the early 1990's. Professor Barber's first tool looks at a description of the President as passive or active pertaining to his work. (Does the President have a high or low level of energy?). The next tool examines how the President reacts towards his job in either a negative or positive way. (Does the President react well towards his job?) When Barber's analysis is applied to the Trump Administration, it is clear President Trump has high energy towards his job. We see him working at odd hours and tweeting early in the morning. President Trump is very "active". Next is whether the President acts or reacts positively or negatively towards his job. I see no question here since President Trump appears to be negative under Barber's test. Nixon was also "active-negative" under Barber's analysis. We see a current President who is constantly complaining about others. He does not appear to be a happy President. Did you ever notice how the blame seems to fall on someone else?

President Trump is different. In his case he has not been forced into the environment as most Presidential Leaders have in the past, but has created it. This changes my view or approach used to study Presidential Character. When one is thrown into a crisis and one reacts to lead the county the survivor is easy to judge. A good result is a plus, and a bad result is a negative. When one creates the crisis, and reacts to one's own creation, the survivor is not as easy to judge. This is called the Art of the Diversion. If one creates a diversion to alter appearances, then one's actions are surely judged quite differently from one's pure reactions to disasters. One who creates the diversion does so to make one appear to look good. Thus, the conclusion reached is a pretext. It is what magician's call an illusion. Said action creates an illusory conclusion. Under such circumstances, the illusory conclusion amounts to a fake conclusion and the reporting of such (fake) conclusion is not fake news, but true news. It is almost like trying to trick a jury in a criminal proceeding; once the jurors get wind of the attempt to trick them, the jury sees through it and all bets are off. When the President tries to trick the American People into believing he is doing a good job, sooner or later they will see right through it. Is there a better way to describe this? Sure, it is like the student who has his mother write his term paper for him. The student tries to trick the teacher. Once caught, the fraudulent work is recognized for what it is, and the student is punished.

In President Trump's case, it is much simpler than that explanation. His attempts to trick the American People are nothing more than evidence of a character flaw. When Nixon tried to do it, he was called "Tricky Dicky". It is what President Richard Nixon had-a character flaw. Nixon, (like Trump,) thought he was above the law because he was President. By being elected the head of the Executive Branch, the President represents the law by being the Chief Constitutional Officer in charge with its execution and enforcement. Any leader who thinks the law only applies to others, like Trump does and Nixon did, and not to himself, is clearly a flawed thinker. That way of thinking is clearly a violation of the President's oath of office. Thus, such thinking illustrates a character flaw. People who think this way lack the moral integrity or compass to carry out the duties of the Oval Office. This type of harm is toxic to the Oval Office.

When we try to propose a theory of Presidential Character for Donald Trump, we must keep in mind that we must not fall into the trap described. This trap, or character flaw, has much to do with moral fitness. I am tired of hearing President Trump say that "conflicts of interest" do not apply to him. Appearances of Impropriety apply to everyone in all walks of life. Common sense dictates that certain things simply do not look good. When we continue doing things that jeopardize peoples' faith in our position, we harm the reputation of that position. (Watergate Break-in and Clinton-sex scandals.) When you are President of the United States of American, and when you do not care to understand that ethics apply to you, you then illustrate an ignorance that shakes the very foundation of that Great Office. The President is the "Role Model" for America and the Free World. This is a tragedy of great consequence. It is an ongoing harm and not one of a single event or occurrence. It dwarfs the Watergate Break In. The ongoing harm aspect of both Presidents' actions continue to parallel each other. The one crime or error becomes compounded by lies, cover up, and obstruction of justice. Today, we see it in a very clear divisiveness in the United States. We see it in a renewal of hate. We see it in racial bigotry. We see it in racial prejudice. We see it in loss of faith. A

President must unify the country. A President who prides himself on divisiveness is not a United States or World Leader. I believe the character flaw analysis simplifies Professor Barber's analysis. Simple opinion polls validate my conclusion.

It is one thing to try to trick the enemy, and quite another to try to trick the American People. Any President who lies to the American People must understand that his/her days are surely numbered. Now if the American People buy into the lie(s), and overlook the lies(s), then again, the People unfortunately get what they deserve. The whole idea of democracy simply goes out the window. The American People are the ultimate check on Government. If the American People give up that power, then all that is left is tyranny. This is what is meant by the fact that even democracy has the seeds to its own destruction by inaction. This is what we are seeing today. The American People cannot turn a blind eye on their ultimate role of keeping their government accountable. If we have learned any lesson from the Trump Administration, it is this clear, coherent and important lesson. Inaction and complacency encourages tyrannical government.

Is this survival of the fittest? We know it is not. This creates a new focus of analysis for purposes of a theory of Presidential Character. I suppose if one can control the situation, one can then control the outcome. The problem is that life is not that simple. We have an era of fake news, fake issues, and fake conclusions. I suppose this is a new era of "fake" government. The American People deserve much better as long as they do their part. Further, the above comments refer to domestic policy and not foreign policy primarily because the average citizen does not know what his/her vital security interests are. That fact creates concern for all Americans. The problem is simply that

President Trump fails to know what America's vital security interests are. This problem magnifies our safety and security concerns as our President tries to go the foreign policy route all alone. Foreign Policy and Safety and Security Issues are much bigger than the President and must be implemented to survive long after the President's replacement or death. United States Foreign Policy is currently fragmented and incoherent. Our vital security interests are at risk. Our country could be in grave danger under the current Administration. I wish the American People would understand that point.

The Bush and Clinton years provided many sparks for debate both on the domestic and foreign policy fronts. The Department was thriving during those years and the students were clearly much better than those in my first classes. The University was thriving and becoming more culturally diverse. This was evidenced by better classroom discussion, better essay performance and better testing performance.

I also improved during these times. I decided that in order to help students, I would prepare model answers after all tests given. I wanted to help students in ways other professors did not. I wanted to make the class better. I would also place old tests with model answers on reserve at the library for students to study from for midterms and finals. After each test given, I would prepare a model answer and would tell the students to keep their tests after they answered their questions alerting them that I would provide them with model answers they could use to study from for the final. This allowed the students to have an outline for the course. I would also place their test and model answer on reserve at the library.

I would only prepare model answers after reading all of the class' tests. In this way, when I responded to the questions, I would also comment on points brought up by students that I did not anticipate. Often, I would read tests with answers creatively using the materials I overlooked. I would respond in all model answers delineating these points to my students. This approach made me a better teacher and made my students better performers. This symbiosis was clear, alive and dynamic.

Throughout my thirty years at Southern, I always placed old tests and model answers on reserve from prior years to help my students prepare for their tests. I also would place an edition of our textbook on reserve for those students who could not, through any fault of their own, afford the book. I would also place all written handouts given in class on reserve for those students who may have missed class for one reason or another. These steps taken were simply a few ways I tried to make the class better for my students and to help them. I believe it did make a difference for many students and I hopefully showed them that taking the extra effort to review these tests was well worth it in the end. Of course, every year when I received my evaluations back from the students, I saw some students' appreciative and other students' critical. I made the extra effort and it was done for those students who felt it beneficial. For those that got upset, they simply did not take advantage of the opportunity. In any event, teaching always continued to be a learning process for me as well as for my students. I was often told by my students that they really enjoyed the class. That made me feel good because I felt the same way.

Regarding the teacher evaluations, I would always review them. I always looked for constructive criticism so I could improve in areas students thought deficient. I would always request that my students be constructive in their criticism. Some would say, "I hated the course, and he was the worst teacher I ever had." (Ouch!) The problem I would experience is that those students would never say what specifically was so bad, and what exactly they hated. I would try to tell students early on, that if it is a poor choice of book, or poor instruction, that said comments are truly constructive and should be stated with particularity. I learned to express my concerns to students so they would not continue to evaluate in unusual and/or improper ways. I would also tell them that constructive criticism is good and benefits both students and teachers.

The most constructive criticism I received over the years had to do with the writing requirement. I found it best to place those requirements in writing. Although I would go over the requirements in class, sometimes students would miss out, come in late, or just not pay attention. As a result, some students would hand in deficient term papers. This really was not a big deal because all my students were given the benefit of a re-write if they chose to improve their papers. The only condition I placed on the students in this regard was that the papers be submitted on time. In this way, I could read all of the papers, make constructive criticisms, and hand them back for revisions. In any event, I found it best to always place the instructions clearly in writing so students could see them, digest them, and then question me in class about them. I would tend to forget that students, like everyone else, have other coursework to prepare and other issues and problems that needed to be addressed. Time management is key and is hard to effectively deal with when students feel overwhelmed. This issue becomes more difficult and compounded by personal and family problems that come into the mix. The key is to be as clear as one can on the syllabus. This way students tend to become aware early in the class about the class requirements and the Professor's expectations. This makes for a clear transparent semester. Clear sailing is the aim. In my thirty years, I am glad to say most of my sailing was clear sailing. Every once and a while though, there were some storms, but we navigated through them. The storms made us all a little bit stronger. After all, Teacher/Student adaptation is always a beneficial part of learning.

Chapter Six: Laughter is
the Best Medicine.

Humor is a universal language. (Joel Goodman) Humor is the great thing, the saving

thing. The minute it crops up, all our irritation and resentments slip away, and a sunny

spirit takes their place. (Mark Twain) Humor is mankind's greatest blessing. (Mark

Twain). To make others laugh and smile are two of God's greatest gifts to man. (Me).

Although I may have taken the time machine and digressed at times, one objective/

purpose of this book is to share some funny situations I have experienced both in and

out of class. Learning to laugh, even at ourselves, makes the journey fun, worthwhile

and rewarding. The fun times are the memorable times; the bad times are the forgettable

times. Students appreciate an atmosphere conducive to learning. Laughter creates that

atmosphere. No one likes being in class with a sour puss. If you are a sour puss, you

should not be teaching. I always tried to abide by that rule. No one wants to be

remembered as a sour puss. I surely did not want to be remembered that way.

During my first year at Southern, I recall having a police officer in one of my U.S.

Government sections. If my memory serves me correctly, he was either on the

Bridgeport, Stratford, or Trumbull Police Department. The gentleman participated in

class and was a real pleasure to have in class. He contributed things about his job that

truly made the class interesting. The Officer evidently enjoyed my class because

he told Jean how much he liked the class. Jean was kind enough to share his comments.

He liked the fact that it was not just lecture but class discussion. He also liked the fact

that if students would not participate, I would call on them. This was 1987 or 1988.

Fast forward to 2010 in the time machine. I am now teaching a law class entitled U.S. Legal Systems. I believe the class met from 5 to 6:20 p.m. but it could have been a two-and a half hour class meeting only once a week. At the end of one class, the gentleman, (I was referring to earlier) who now is retired, about twelve years later, shows up at my class and introduces me to his daughter who is now taking this class. I guess as a joke, he stated to me that well you taught me and now my daughter, so I guess you may be teaching my grandchildren next. Oh my God, this reminded me of "Goodbye, Mr. Chips". This event may not appear funny but it gets better. While at Southern, I remember this happening to me all of three or four times. They aren't saying goodbye to me, they are saying hello again and again. The problem is if I'm Mr. Chips, I guess I am the stale version of Mr. Chips at that. How could all these years have passed? How am I still here (I wondered) after all of these years? How could dad refer me to his daughter? What if she hated me or my class? I hope I got better with age. I was embarrassed. I felt like a bottle of wine or a stale potato chip. It is abundantly clear that when I started at Southern I was thirty-two years old. When I retired, I was now sixty-two years old. In a span of thirty years, six Presidents later give or take, and about thirty pounds heavier, I was still around. I taught thousands of students. I state this because when many of my colleagues laugh they will hear me say: "Your day too is coming".

On a lighter note, though, I must say that the thirty years went by so fast. I enjoyed every second of every minute of every hour of every day I spent at Southern. The School, the Students, the Administration, the whole ball of wax was by far the most

99

precious parts for my experience. I cannot state one regret. Out of all my jobs and all of my life experiences, there are none more precious to me and these times at Southern. This is the God's Honest Truth. All I can say is that I hope sincerely that all of my students and my colleagues have the same feelings and experiences I mention. I guess some journeys are wonderful like that. They simply touch us in very special ways. I suppose it is similar to a type of Grace from God if we are fortunate enough to receive and appreciate it. It is truly the definition of what is meant by being "Blessed". How else can I explain it. Possibly, "heaven on earth", almost like Nonie's spaghetti. How else does somebody describe heaven on earth? It is like heaven on earth. It is truly special. Words have no other explanation for it. It is simply the best there is. It compares to all the wonderful emotions, like love, joy and/or friendship. The three mentioned are very close indeed. Blessed by God is the best characterization I can give it. I do hope others feel the same way. It is a truly beautiful feeling. The experience makes it all worthwhile.

Next, was one situation I will never forget. I was teaching a class called Administrative Law. The class included many older students who work full-time. I always would try to be lenient with students coming in late knowing that often they were caught in traffic, or were late arriving from work, etc. I would ask the students if they were late to try to come in quietly and not to disturb the other students in class.

One night when class ended, I noticed that a student evidently fell asleep in the back of the room. Often after class, students would approach me to ask questions about the class or their assignment, or if they came in late about what they might have missed. I recall standing at the front of the class with two students speaking to me. The first students says someone fell asleep in the back of the room. (Like I did not know that). The professor who teaches after my class then comes into the classroom and looks at me and says: " Cannatelli, by God, I think you killed him". I guess he implied that my class was so boring that the student died of boredom. Well, the students in the front of the classroom both said at the same time in unison, "No, he can't be dead- don't worry professor, he's snoring". We all had a chuckle. (ha, ha, ha). Although I did not think this to be funny at all, the people there laughed out loud. (LOL). This is a true story. Lucky for me I didn't kill him, I just put him to sleep.

Boy, some days you just can't win. By the way, the student never woke up when we left. No autopsy was needed. I wonder what type of murder I would have been charged with? Monotonous Manslaughter in the first degree. This could be an episode out of "Monk".

Every October or so, the Political Science Department would sponsor a trip to New York (or Boston) to the Law School Forum which hosts many of the ABA approved Law Schools throughout the country. I was the Prelaw adviser years later, but this particular year the honors went to my colleague Art Paulson. Art invited me to go along for company to help with the ten or twelve students who signed up.

Now Art is a nice guy who I always recall (seeing him) riding his bike to school. He would ride in the rain, the snow, and I would always worry about him. He was/is a no-nonsense type of person and very funny. He enjoys life and has a great sense of humor. He and his wife Carolyn are such lovely people. Carolyn has Art beat when it comes to humor. She often would make fun of Art in a cute way, which made everyone laugh. (I recall, for example, how Lynn was telling me how she and Art had to catch a plane or train early the next morning. "When we woke up", she stated, "Art noticed the water company had the road blocked off on our street. Art, upon noticing this, ran outside in his pajamas to talk to the workmen hoping we could leave". We all laughed because everyone could just picture Art running outside and doing that.

Well one year back in the nineties, Art and I hosted the students. We rode down on the train to the forum. Upon arriving in New York, we would walk from Grand Central to the hotel sponsoring the forum. Well, one year, I took my paralegal Don, and Art and I sponsored about ten or eleven students as already mentioned. This year we arrived in New York early, so we decided to have lunch before we headed over to the Law School Forum (which was walking distance away). Art, as we walked, would assign numbers to the students so we would hear, "one, two, three," etc., almost like being in boy scout camp or the army, so we all kept track of each other in an effort to not lose anyone. On this particular trip we got to the restaurant and ate and then proceeded to leave. We spend the entire day at the forum and then walked to the train station. When we were getting ready to leave, one of the students asked, "Where's Evelyn"? Art, and I looked at each other, and noticed that Evelyn was not with us. At that moment Art panics and decides to send me back with the students while he decides to trace steps backwards in an effort to find Evelyn.

Later that night, I phoned Art. He could not find Evelyn. Well, as time passed, Don, my paralegal was able to speak with Evelyn. She was evidently upset stating that she went to the lady's room and when she returned we were all gone. She was upset. Oh boy! I guess Art and I were upset too, because we simply did not miss her until later on that day, despite the counting which we evidently failed to do once in New York. What a freaking nightmare. "One, Two, Three, oh let it be". This is what we mean by diversity, we take our students to New York and lose them. To this day, I don't know how we did that. It was almost like the blind leading the blind. We vowed that this must never happen again. It hasn't. But could you imagine how something could have occurred? We were so fortunate that nothing bad happened to Evelyn. As I think back I can see how it might appear funny now, but it was not so funny when it happened. I remember mentioning it to Art, and he and I would both look at each other and roll our eyes. What a royal nightmare-Ugh! Law School forum somehow obtained a bad connotation after that day.

One of the coolest things about teaching law is the way I could and did use my experience in Court to explain certain legal concepts. In U.S. Legal Systems, or PSC 321-01, I would constantly be asked about certain legal doctrines and how the doctrines applied in real life. One chapter dealt with the "Powers of the Court", and included the "Contempt Power". One student asked me to explain how it works. I relayed how contempt can occur either in the presence of the Court, or outside of the presence of the Court. The student asked again, stating "I really don't understand".

I then said, "well, I can remember being held in contempt once". "When it happens to you, it is not something you forget very quickly" I said. You could now hear a pin drop in the classroom. The student asked, "could you tell us what happened"? I said "sure, are you ready"? The entire class perked up for my response clearly hoping I was thrown in jail. There is nothing better than when the entire class looks up and listens.

Well, one day I had a sentencing scheduled for a Defendant I represented to be heard at 11a.m. sharp before the Honorable Stuart M. Schimelman. Judge Schimelman was a short guy who really put up with little or no nonsense in his court room. I mean that to the letter. On my way to Court this particular day, I was stopped in the hallway by another Judge, Dale Radcliffe. Judge Radcliffe started asking me about a case or two I was handling (that he was familiar with) and the conversation was not an ex-parte communication with a judge because the questions pertained to cases not being heard by this particular judge. Anyhow, this communication between us took about ten to fifteen minutes and as I scuttled in before Judge Schimelman he was now on the bench and quite annoyed with me for being late. This fact was clear from the Judicial Authority's face. I knew this was not a good sign for me or for my client.

"Mr. Cannatelli, could you explain to me why you are late?" asked the Hon. Judge Schimelmen. I really did not think much about being late, as Judge Radcliffe had just entered the court room behind me and sat down in the back. I surely expected and thought he would come to my aid. Well, as I waited for my savior, the Honorable Dale Radcliffe to ask permission to speak on my behalf, I soon realized that this was a dream that was simply not realistic. How dare he? Well, he dared alright. I was sunk.

I said I did not realize I was so late. The Court stated, "Well a fine is in order". "I order you to pay the clerk $25.00 for your tardiness". I looked up and smiled. I said, but

"Your Honor, surely you can do better than that". I evidently caught the Judicial

Authority off guard. He looked up and appeared annoyed. "Ok", responded the Judicial

Authority. "I fine you $50". My response, "With all due respect, C'mon your Honor, I

know you really can do better than that". The judge roared, "Mr. Cannatelli, you're on

very tenuous grounds". "Fifty Dollars is nothing for such a grave violation as making

this Honorable Court wait", I uttered. The Court slammed me for $100. I stated

"I knew you could do it", and said "thank you, your honor". Schimelman, looked at

me a little confused and just smiled. I really don't know if he ever learned why I was

late. I did not care. Ladies and Gentlemen, but that is an example of the Court's use of

the Contempt Power. The class roared. "Why did you push him", I was asked. I stated,

"because I was right" and Judge Radcliffe was wrong for not coming forward". That was

the best $100 I ever paid. To this day when I see the Hon. Judge Schimelman, he smiles.

He will never forget that moment. I recall seeing him while he sat in New London, so

I stopped by to see him while he as on the bench. He looked up at me and smiled. As

I proceeded to leave, I smiled and waved. He waived back while sitting on the bench.

We both enjoyed the moment as we thought back to that solemn day. From being a

very serious matter, it turned out to be a laugh and war story we would both recall for

a very long time.

I think the Judge realized that my being late was not my fault. He realized

that I could take it with the best of them. He is an example of a good judge. Why did

I him? I pushed him because I was not the cause of my being late. I pushed him because

105

sometimes justice is blind. I pushed him so I would be able to communicate with you a little about the Contempt Power. The student said, "next time, just give me the $25.00". We all laughed. I said, "next time, you all will be bailing me out". One student yelled, "Don't you hold your breath on that". We all laughed and continued on with the class. It was a precious moment. It was funny. It was a unique moment I could share because of my legal experience. The experience allowed me to enrich my class.

There was another time that Dr. Rai asked if he could sit in one of my classes. I believe the School and the Department wanted to make sure the new professors were properly monitored and doing their job. I said I welcomed his attendance. The Department and staff were always courteous and would announce their presence ahead of time. This was nice and I would have expected an unannounced visit to better evaluate my teaching abilities. Anyhow, Dr. Rai did come to class on a particular day while I was instructing my United States Government class.

Dr. Rai comes in and sits in the center of the class while class is in session. I recalled this particular day very vividly. As he comes in, one of my students asks me a question about affirmative action and as he asked the question Dr. Rai was placing his lunch and thermos underneath his seat. I knew at the time that Kul was writing a book on the subject, so I stated that perhaps that question could be addressed by Dr. Rai. Well, Dr. Rai unfortunately was not paying attention and when I deferred to him, he looked up as if he was gasping for air. You know, we all have been there, when the teacher asks us a question and we are not paying attention. The class roared. Kul was looking up in wonder how he got himself embroiled into this discussion when he just came into the room. He looked perplexed and confused. We all smiled at Dr. Rai's response. The class roared. I could not help but laugh because of the expression on his face; it was worth a million dollars. He looked like he had seen a ghost. After class, Kul said to me "I am not coming to your class again". We both laughed so hard I thought I was going to hurt my ribs. I realized that my colleagues were unique people. In hindsight, I really never meant to put him on the spot. It just turned out that way. Boy was it funny though. I think he felt-set up. (Like I told the class beforehand what to do). That simply was not the case. It was a hilarious moment. I wonder if Kul will remember that time in class.

Dr. Rai and I would often discuss the political issue whether "Affirmative Action" had/has outlived its usefulness. Kul seemed to think it had. With my experience practicing law, I unfortunately disagreed. Kul would ask me why. I could only say that as long as I see discrimination in society, my belief is that there will be a need for "Affirmative Action". I often see it in jails in Connecticut where inmates who are handicapped are not adequately accommodated. I see it with HUD policies and other federal programs violating the Connecticut Constitution when utilized or implemented to segregate people. I can go on and on. I am sorry to say that discrimination is active in society, so I must and do respectfully disagree. Anyhow, Dr. Rai and I would disagree in a respectful way. Who is correct? I suppose we may both be correct. The Democrats and Republicans still disagree on this issue. I do not see an answer any time soon. I do know with the large number of police shootings many minority citizens feel discrimination is rampant. It really does not matter whether the discrimination is institutional or not. If it exists, society and the law must do more to eradicate it.

Further, President Trump's treatment of transgendered people keeps the issue alive. I suppose we are lucky to have the Courts. They are the last bastion of hope for those discriminated against in this country.

Those were a few of the many stories I recall. There are many more. Keep in mind that the funny stories are also ones that are never forgotten. What tends to happen is that we are often reminded of them by occurrences in everyday life. We see something that causes our memories to think back and then we recall. This is one of the great things about teaching. Once we recall, we step back and tell the class about these stories which add fun and flavor to the class. Each story has a moral or objective. It must be relevant to the course obviously. Funny stories are placed to the top of the list.

Without laughter education suffers. People perform better when the pressure is off. Class should never be pressure cooker. It must be an atmosphere conducive to thinking and learning. That atmosphere has to include the many funny experiences we endured throughout our lives. It makes the experience enjoyable for all. It teaches by example. Examples reinforce learning. That is why reasoning by example reinforces memory. This is not studying by example, it is reasoning by example. Examples aid our memories such that studying is limited. Reasoning is learned. It is not really studied. Examples help students reason, which then help them learn. I guess I am simply saying that things studied are often forgotten, while things reasoned are often remembered.

Chapter Seven: Problems with
Resolutions for New Professors

I now consider some of the problems I noticed at Southern that will always continue to be present for both new and old teachers alike. I discuss them to help with an easy resolution. My intent is to help and not to trivialize the problems. Some seem small but if ignored will be a constant source of irritation and aggravation.

Classroom Management: I know some of you will read this and say this topic is irrelevant to college. I disagree for many of the following reasons.

Prior to teaching a class, the professor must do some truly basic things. For example, he or she must choose the book(s). Common sense dictates reviewing the book before selection. Even if the teacher is selected at the last minute and the book has been selected by someone else, I would suggest still reviewing it. I believe that preparation is key. Even if the book is forced down your throat, the teacher should be aware of this pitfall and correct the situation in the future even if the book is simply your poorest choice. If I have a book I don't like, I supplement it with hand-outs and correct the deficiencies. You would do the same and explain to the class the issue so the students are aware of your concern and action. Always be open and honest with your students.

The first class I would discuss disciplinary matters. For example, I would tell my students that we must not talk at the same time. If you have a question please raise your hand and I promise to call on you. I would also discuss the protocol for arriving late. Come in quietly do not talk and do not interrupt the class. Anyhow, once I discussed the do's and don'ts and everyone appeared to be on the same page,

I would then start the material. Please note that the basics are basics and apply to all.

There are a few cardinal sins I must mention. On the first day of class, the Professor should not only be there, but should be in class - ON TIME. I say this because if you want to give a good impression to your students, there is no better way to do this than to lead by example. If you are always late for class, you have really no legitimate right to criticize those students who simply follow your poor example. Also, try not TO MISS THE FIRST DAY OF CLASSES. Boy is that a terrible thing to do. I remember one year that my colleague, Art, missed his first day of classes. Jean, our beloved secretary, never let him forget it. Art was the most conscientious professor ever to teach at Southern. He never let that happen again. This is not a good way to start off the class. So please do not miss your first day of classes.

Finally, I guess I am over-stressing the importance of simply starting the race with two feet on the ground. The prepared professor is the better model. Always being prepared means always being a role model for your students. I always would try my best. Keep in mind that we all have faults and do make mistakes. When I made them, I would apologize to the class and immediately take responsibility for my mistakes. This shows honesty and integrity and generates honesty and integrity. We must be accountable. Accountability is a big part of education and of life.

Next, I always prepared a syllabus which included all the important things a student should know. I always included: contact information; book and author information; test information; course requirements; dos and don'ts. Many professors are clear on how

110

important this is. The syllabus is a contract. If properly prepared, it clearly informs the students of their Substantive and Procedural Due Process Rights under the Fourteenth Amendment to the United States Constitution. The syllabus should contain basically all the information students need to successfully take and complete your class. It should include all course requirements. It should include the number of tests and paper requirements, if any. It should include goals of the course as communicated by the professor or the course description. Without attempting to beat a dead cat, I cannot stress how much toil and aggravation can be avoided by a well-planned syllabus. Early on, the professor should also go over the syllabus in order to alert the students of the teacher's expectations and past experiences dealing with the subject matter and prior student issues. This can and will often avoid similar problems from creeping up again.

For example, I taught U.S. Government for over thirty years. My course requirements included two tests and a research paper. On the first day of class, I made it a point to go over everything with the students, addressing any and all of questions. First, I would introduce myself. Second, I would show the students the book. Third, I would tell the students that I would place a copy of the book on reserve at the library for those students who could not afford the book, or for those students who could not purchase one because of a delay in financial aid, or because the book store failed to order or have enough books on hand. I immediately would develop a rapport with my students. This was the way I clarified all questions and aimed at reaching a meeting of the minds. This worked quite well for over thirty years. Further, the syllabus should be emailed to students prior to class and the professor should have hard copies for those students who register late, or simply do not get one electronically.

School Cancellations: I have more often than not got up on snowy mornings, listened to the news for cancellations, and hearing of none, then proceeded to Southern only to learn that school had been canceled after my leaving home.

You see, because I am a practicing attorney, I would often request the early morning class, or 8:10 am to 9:00 am. This would mean that I would get up early and leave the house by 7:00 am to get to school on time. I recall one year getting to school and going to class with thirty students there. The janitor, Mack, knocked on the door to tell us that school had been canceled. This is terrible and agonizing to say the least.

Of course, I have also been a part of the faculty who experienced the opposite. We had one President who would cancel school at the bat of an eye. Well, I taught a graduate class in Administrative Law and Public Policy one semester that only met on Monday evenings for two and a half hours. That class got canceled four time in one semester. I was able to salvage the loss class-time by discussions on Black Board. Sometimes, you simply cannot win. Four three-hour class cancellations are a death blow.

Advice: Like the old boy scout motto, "always be prepared". Plan for the worst and instruct your class for the contingency of missing class. After all, you are the one who is responsible for teaching the class. You are the one responsible for getting through the material. The prepared professor will get through completing his or her material. The unprepared professor will fail to competently get through the material thereby cheating the students of their education. Thus, be prepared to deal with it intelligently and competently. If you do not, your students will suffer. You then will get the reputation of a slacker. This is not good and is a poor reflection of you and of the school. It was terrible to try to catch up after missing so many classes. We worked hard to do so. Graduate Students, unlike Undergraduate Students, are more in tune with whether their professor is competent or not. Competency is a big deal and is often determined by one's performance while teaching.

MISSING CLASSES: Great teachers do not miss class. Professors are like all other teachers and are role models for their students. Absent some emergency, the Professor should not miss class. At Southern, if the Professor knows that he/she will not be available on a specific date, the proper protocol is to inform the class of the date and time that class will be canceled, and the instructor should give the class a pending assignment. We must not cheat our students. Plan and provide for the contingency. The Professor must do that always; he/she must always be prepared.

ADVICE: When I had to miss class, I would often give the class a take-home exam, and would notify both the Department Secretary and Department Head. In thirty years, I do not believe I canceled class more than five times either due to severe illness or something of that nature. At Southern, we really do not cancel classes for the heck of it. We pride ourselves on being prepared for class and anxious to be a part of Southern's mission. Like Rolls Royce(s), we pretty much don't break down. We are reliable and proud to be here for our students. In fact, I can often remember students complaining to me that unlike other course teachers, I have not canceled class once. I would say, "I know" with a coy smile.

113

TARDY STUDENTS: As a teacher, I would experience students coming to class late. This could be a problem. If one student keeps coming in late and the teacher ignores it, this often will lead to a chain reaction. Oh, the guy's a pushover kind of thing, so I will get there when I get there. What do you do? Do you play hardball, or let it go? Keep in mind, you're damned if do, and damned if you don't. You walk a fine line and call it as you see it. Some students cannot be on time due to work, etc.

ADVICE: The Professor is in charge of classroom-management. Now it is true, college students are not grade-school students. I would state certain ground rules to my students. I would tell the students, if you come in late, all I ask is that you come in quietly and try not to talk while I am instructing. If a handout was given while you were not present, do not, I repeat, do not come forward requesting it and interrupt the class. I suggest this because otherwise you will have people coming in late, talking, and coming up one at a time for handouts not really caring they are interrupting classroom-instruction. Now, if you allow that kind of thing, it is on you. Remember, you are in charge. What you say goes. You are responsible for your class. If you are a pushover, then you get what you deserve; (A classroom full of students who are mismanaged and chaotic). If that is the environment you allow, I simply wish you good luck. You will need it, I assure you.

CELL PHONES AND COMPUTERS: These devices, if used properly are good educational assets. The problem arises when students are texting their friends and not paying attention. Often a student will tell you that he/she is taking notes on their computer. As you walk by, you see him/her on the internet or Facebook or what-have -you. What do you do? Storm out? Yell and scream? Ignore it? Plead? Well no. You have to deal with it now better than later. If you ignore it, it simply will not go away. It simply gets bigger. It will haunt you. The monster will grow (if you will). It grows inside you and around you. Once it gets too big, it becomes unmanageable. You must deal with it as soon as possible. It does not pay to procrastinate.

ADVICE: The professor is in charge of classroom-management. If you see people not paying attention because they are texting, you remind them very calmly that they are annoying you and to please leave the class to text. Remind them that cell phones really are not part of the class. It is disrespectful to text or to talk on the phone during class. If it happens the first time, they will be given a warning. If it happens a second time, they will be given a second warning. If it happens a third time, they will be asked to leave the class. Usually, when a student is asked to leave for that particular class, he/she will not offend again. I am stating this as fact from experience.

Usually, at the start of the semester, the Professor can and should explain his/her concerns to the students who normally agree to comply. Discretion is the better part of valor. It does not do any good to yell, stomp, or leave class. Keep in mind that it is your job to maintain a cool, calm atmosphere which is conducive to learning. You should also keep in mind that this will always be an issue for the teacher and student in the modern classroom. After all, it is the information age. Technology is everywhere. I usually try to call on the offending student and that wakes him/her up to my concerns. If it continues, I try to handle it in a matter-of-fact way. If you show too much alarm, it is not good. It is a better approach to simply try to be as professional as you can. Remember that you are dealing with adults and not children. Try not to forget that point. Often, the offending party is an adult attending classes who is older and wiser. Often, the offending party may have a lapse in judgment. Just keep in mind that your issue is one that all Professors have to be concerned about. The sooner you deal with it, the better it is for you to instruct and for your students to learn. Remember, that "this too shall pass". Discretion is the better part of valor. Be kind, respectful and firm but fair.

MISSED TESTS AND MISSED WORK: One of the biggest issues I had with students was their constantly missing scheduled tests and assignments by due dates. I noticed that some of my colleagues did not seem as concerned about this as I did. I hate it when someone would get an unfair advantage over someone else. I would see this happening again and again. I always felt it was my job to level the playing field. This was a hard job to master. The test is to be given on a certain date and the syllabus requires students knowing they cannot make a specific date to give prior notice to the teacher. This truly sounds good in theory, but works poorly in practice. What to do about this issue?

This gets crazy when it happens to be a mid-term. If you are too easy going, you will be allowing students to take the test whenever they feel like it. That is unfair to the rest of the students who are prepared to take the test on time. I suppose an exception can be made for a true emergency. I learned that those few who usually have a problem early on are the chosen few who always have a problem. It usually gets worse over time. This is not good. The best advice is to learn early those students who always have excuses. It

116

normally occurs with the same (few) individuals.

ADVICE: You have to be firm but fair. The teacher is expected to deal with the problem in a way that does not penalize those students who are prepared and who get their work in on time. For example, if someone misses the midterm and has a good reason, it might be alright to permit a student to take a makeup which is a bit harder (or requires a bit more work). Normally, I would request a reason for the student's missing the test to begin with. If the student has a good reason, of course I would try to accommodate him/her. The problem arises when the student has a mediocre reason. Clearly, he or she missed the exam because he/she was not prepared or simply did not feel like taking the test. The student thinks you are there to serve him/her, and you have nothing better to do than to accommodate him/her regarding the make-up. It is your job, right? WRONG. This has become a serious problem primarily because teachers have bent over backwards to permit this sort of thing. This is a serious problem. Easy-going teachers foster bad habits with their students. Further, catering to those who are lazy harms those students in their later real-life pursuits. I was tough in this regard because I was concerned about being fair to all my students and not fostering lazy habits.

One reason a student attends college is to prepare the student for the real world. I explained this time and time again, that no employer wants employees who are not dependable. It is always important to be on time and to be prepared. In the real world, often the person who is hired is not the person best qualified for the job. It is often the person who is reliable and dependable. These lessons are often difficult to learn. They should be a part of the educational process. Work must be completed competently, efficiently and timely. There are simply no excuses. You get the job done period.

I had one student who failed to hand in his term paper. The writing requirement was worth forty percent of the grade. He came to my office to discuss it with me. His name was Matthew. Matt comes in and sits down. He asked me if I would allow him to slide on the term paper. I looked at him a little confused and wondered why he thought I would permit him to do that. I looked at him, and said," Matt, you do not appear to be in a coma. You seem to be healthy. You do not give me the impression that you are dying. Why in God's world would I assign a writing requirement to the entire class, all whom have done their papers, and out of the blue, simply let you slide? Does that seem fair? Does it sound reasonable to you? Have you ever heard that I have done that before?" What possibly were you thinking when you decided to ask me that?

Matt looked at me and was clearly embarrassed." Good", I thought to myself. I stated to Matt that I would give him the courtesy I give to all other students. If and when I am ready to post my grades, I see that your grade is missing the term paper, I will give you an incomplete which permits you until the end of the next semester to complete the paper. If not completed by the end of the next semester, the University Record's Office then converts all incomplete grades to an "F". I shook Matt's hand and that was that. The situation irritated me. I never forgot it. I believe he did get his paper in. I believe he also told others that my class was the best class he ever took at Southern. After that meeting, I recall very specifically what I did. I recalled earlier that week knocking on the Honorable Richard Comerford's door of his chambers, as I had a pretrial with him in a criminal matter. As I entered with the state's attorney, Maxine Wilensky, I saw Judge Comerford reading the Bible. I did not comment, but thought a lot about that later on. Evidently Judge Comerford had a sentencing that day and was truly troubled over it. He had a tough decision to make. He struggled with it. He needed quiet and clarity of thought. He prayed. He asked for help. He meditated. I mention this because it is very significant. It illustrates how good people need insight. How good people try to always do the right thing. (That was a thing the late-great Hon. Judge Richard Damiani would always say.) I realized at that moment, that I was being tested. I was quite upset and probably felt like Judge Comerford when he was reading the bible. Well, I did not have a Bible, but did have a prayer in mind. It was called the Prayer of St. Francis of Assisi, my Patron Saint. The prayer is significant and reads:

> Lord, make me an instrument of your peace,
> Where there is hatred, let me sow love;
> Where there is injury, pardon;
> Where there is doubt, faith;
> Where there is despair, hope;
> Where there is darkness; light;
> Where there is sadness, joy;
>
> O Divine Master, grant that I may not so much seek to be consoled
>
> at to console;
> To be understood, as to understand;
> To be loved at to love.
>
> For it is giving that we receive;
> It is in pardoning that we are pardoned;
> And it is in dying that we are born to eternal life.

I guess I was bothered by Matt's request. Did I give him the impression I would do this? Maybe I was so easy going that I appeared to foster his attempt to beat the system?

Maybe I should have said, fine. I simply couldn't do it. I knew if I had allowed him to slide, that it would have bothered me to the day I died. The prayer helped me realize it was just part of the job. Students try to get over, no big deal. It is nothing personal. Get over it and move on. Interesting to note, about six months later, I asked the Judge about the prayer he liked. The one I mentioned was one he said he often recited. What a coincidence. I suppose we can never give up on our students. They often will put us to the test. Just as we test them, they test us. We must often learn from them. In learning, we must always try, "to do the right thing", no matter how difficult the right thing is.

To clarify, one of the hardest things teachers endure is the part of the job that entails soul searching. It happens very often when you teach. For example, it happens every time you put a grade on a student's record. It happens whenever a tragic event happens in a student's life. It happens whenever you attempt to curve a test. It happens whenever your grade appears to work an enduring hardship on a student due to no fault of the student. It happens when a student misreads a final and although batting an "A", only does 50% of the final test. The saga goes on and on. Like all professions, make no mistake about it, teachers have to soul search. It looks easy but is not easy at all.

How do we recognize these issues? They are the ones we cannot stop thinking about. It is like a jury in a criminal matter where one member refrains from voting guilty while all the others are clear the defendant is in fact guilty. It is a hesitancy. It is a real doubt we have and entertain whether or not we are doing the right thing. It may cause you to lose sleep. It is a recurrent thought that will not go away. It is our conscience. Good teachers are aware of this. It is like a sixth sense. Good teachers embrace it and deliberate hard to overcome it. Good teachers make the hard decisions fairly and uniformly, with an eye to equity and fairness. I can only call it soul searching. It includes the calling to do right. That calling may be wrong in other situations, but not here. Once the decision is made, and if the right thing is not done, it haunts you day in and day out until the day you die (or for a very long time). This role of the Professor cannot be overlooked. It is a distinctive role which is alive and well. It is by-far the measuring rod we use. That measuring rod is more often than not, subjective. It is subjective in the sense that we cannot fool ourselves about our own decisions. We are accountable to none other than ourselves in this regard. Shakespeare said it best: "to thine own self be true". Usually our standards used are objective, but we must never forget that our own personal idiosyncrasies also come into play. The balance must always be a delicate one. This particular challenge is the hardest one of all.

Chapter Eight: Errors I Made
and Lessons I Learned.

DISABILITY RESOURCES

As mentioned earlier, when the Professor prepares the class syllabus, he/she should have information pertaining to the disability resource office and staff. Students who need an accommodation should meet with the disability resource center and should provide the instructor with information pertaining to proper accommodations for the student.

I erred by having the information on the syllabus, but by not following up in class. This is very important. The professor really needs to verbally communicate with those students seeking class accommodations to follow up with the disability resource center. One semester I did not orally inform the class and one student, who was in fact registered with the center for his other classes, chose not to inform me he needed an accommodation. He wrote his term paper without seeking accommodations and did not perform very well. I was later told he did not have his accommodation. My issue was simply that I was never made aware of this student's need for accommodations. This is a problem that could have been averted. I was only informed about this from the student's mother. I believe the student might have been embarrassed, but I am not sure. The teacher must inform the class about the disability resource center and should try to speak with students privately so as not to cause embarrassment or alarm. This is very important. Proper accommodations are essential to ensure fair student progress.

The only point I make here is that students could use the center to obtain unfair advantage if not properly monitored. One other problem I realized was that students needing extra time would take their tests at the disability resource center. I noticed students would make their appointment for a specific day and time to take the test and then would take it later whenever they felt like it. I pointed this out to the center that this is again unfair to the other students who take their test on time. In any event, whenever classroom accommodations are required, the professor really needs to monitor the student in order to maintain fairness to all. Accommodations do not mean unfair advantage over others. I learned this later while at Southern. I simply thought that the program monitored this type of situation. Often, the professor could and does drop the ball by simply not monitoring the specifics of what is going on as compared to what is suppose to be going on. Please do not fall into that trap. By a failure to monitor the program, the teacher becomes part of the problem. This is not what the program is devised to accomplish. Again, I mention the need to be firm, but fair. Be careful.

There was one other lesson I learned pertaining to disability resources. This was my error and I am ashamed to mention it, but do so to explain some errors that professors make. I recall teaching two separate sections of United States Government. Once class met at 8:10 a.m., while the other class met at 12:10 p.m. I recall telling my early morning class that if, for some reason they miss the 8 a.m. class, they could take the test at my noon class. I also told the students that they should get my permission a head of time if at all possible. Well, that simple effort to accommodate my earlier class turned into an all-out nightmare. About ten people sought permission to take the test at noon. I agreed. When the noon class came in to take the test, we had to grab seats from an empty class room to accommodate now fifty students, instead of the normal forty. As I was monitoring the test, I notice one of my female students who was assigned to the noon exam and took the class normally at noon, was becoming very sweaty and starting to experience a panic attack. I immediately realized this was due to my allowing so many students into the room. It was hot, stuffy, and this poor girl could not handle it. THIS WAS MY ERROR AND NOT HER'S. In order to mitigate the circumstances, I told the girl to go to the disability resource center to finish her test. She went there and was able to finish her test and did quite well. As I think back, I state very clearly that this fiasco was my doing and my doing alone. Had I gotten upset with the student, she would have probably received an incomplete and all this because of my actions. The only point that I am making here, is that when the error made is that of the professor, he/she must fess up to it and correct it. This was simply not the student's fault. It was my fault. I created the situation. I am lucky that the other students could perform under such stressful conditions. I thank God for having the disability resource center to bail me out of that one. Amen.

ATTENDANCE

The school now has a mandatory attendance policy. This is a good thing. When I came into class, I always had an attendance book I asked the students to sign. I would tell them never to sign anybody's name other than their own. I explained with mandatory reporting that missing classes early-on could result in loss of financial aid.

My mistake would be those people who came in late. They would not come up to sign in, and would eventually be reported absent. The registrar would academically drop these students from the class and I would have to go nuts getting them re-admitted prior to finals. Do not fall into this trap. Alert students of the need to sign in even if they arrive late. This will save time and aggravation later in the last days of your course. Of course, if you get the attendance sheet with the students' pictures on it, it is much easier to learn the students' names early on and it is much easier to note the students' attendance. The teacher really needs to stay on top of attendance for many reasons which will avoid undue hardships later on.

PLAGIARISM

In recent years, I have experienced issues of plagiarism. The University has a protocol for dealing with this very important issue. I had to deal with it a few times. What I did not realize is that it is more common today than it was in the past. I believe this is simply because of the internet and information highway. When I experienced it, I simply would meet with the student, discuss the issue with the student, and would give him/her an "F" on the particular assignment, but would allow him/her to redo the work. I explained that said conduct is an egregious violation of the Scholastic Rules and could result in expulsion. I quite frankly have not experienced all that many violations. I do know that my colleagues have experienced plagiarism violations even at the Graduate level. You would think that by a student's progression to Graduate School that he/she would surely know better than to plagiarize. I believe that when plagiarism occurs at the undergraduate level, that by explaining the dire

125

consequences to the student in conjunction with failing the student assignment, is punishment enough for a single violation. Further, in order to correct the grade, the Student would have to make the work up if the teacher allows him/her to do so.

My problem is that the school allows discretion with the Professor. This is good, but unfortunately has not made the number of incidents decrease. I wonder if my approach is too lenient. Keep in mind that other professors turn the student in to academic affairs. I believe Professors may need more guidance in this area. This is probably a University-wide issue more than a Departmental issue. It is surely a recurring issue and needs clearly mandated policies. It is a tough issue to deal with primarily because of the lack of uniformity in implementation of the rules. Providing the professors with such wide discretion is good, but has its drawbacks when trying to look at fairness of application. "Why should I get turned in to Academic Affairs, when my friend only got a talking to?" As stated before, the implementation of the rules must be firm but fair.

Along with plagiarism are other issues of more minor academic violations. For example, a student should not buy his/her term paper. The student should not have mom or dad write his/her paper. One incident comes to mind that is worth noting. I taught a semester of U.S. Legal Systems. This is a course on the Court System. I would assign cases and ask the students to brief the cases. One semester, I assigned Marbury v. Madison, and told the students I would collect their briefs. Well, one student did not attend the class, but had a friend hand-in his brief. The only problem was that I did not get to the case, so I did not collect the briefs (but took that one). When the next class met, I had in my possession the brief of Jon Smith. I then asked Jon Smith the facts of

Marbury v. Madison without handing back the student his brief.

Needless to say, Jon Smith did not know one fact about the case. This upset me. After calling on him and his inability to recite one fact about the case, I asked Jon to see me after class. It was clear he handed in a brief prepared by someone else.

I explained to Jon and later to the class, that Professors in Law School require their students to brief the assigned cases so the students' will recall the cases not only for class, but for years later. I mentioned how the principle of the case is usually learned and then expanded, retracted, changed, or overruled. I explained that although I had been out of law school for almost forty years, yet I can still remember the first property case I read: Pierson vs Post. The issue was what is property and arose when two hunters shot at a bird or duck and both claimed ownership of the dead prey. The case dealt with property rights to the dead bird or duck. I also explained that if someone carefully reads a case and briefs it, that he/she will recall the facts of the case for years to come. I later asked Jon who prepared the brief he handed in. He knew I was not fooled. I handed the brief back to him and told him to redo it. I explained that if I caught him doing this again, I would fail him in my class. He got the message and did his own work from that day forward. Maybe I was too lenient, but I do not think I was. I made my point, and believe I was firm but fair with Jon. Remember, it was the first assignment for the class. It was not like Jon was doing this all throughout the semester. He simply tried to take a short cut and got caught first. I had no doubt that he learned his lesson from simply getting caught. He learned that the consequences are very serious for this sort of

127

thing. It never happened again.

LAST MINUTE ISSUES

When I first started teaching, I chose to teach classes at ungodly morning hours. As mentioned, I often would teach either early morning classes, or later evening classes. This was simply because I practiced law and had to be in court. Today, with the advent of social media and email, it is easy to cancel class through electronic media. The problem often will arise though when someone gets up and proceeds to school without looking at email. Today most of the students have their email connected to their cell phones so notification is automatic.

I can recall driving to my 6 p.m. class only to get caught in traffic due to an accident. I have an older type of cell phone without internet. As 6 p.m. approached I realized I would not make class. Southern had no protocol for this. In the past, you could simply call the Graduate Admissions Office and someone would run down to tell the class. I phoned the Southern Police Department and pleaded with the dispatcher to have an officer go to inform the class. They did so grudgingly.

I learned from those type of situations. Today when I hand-out the first sign-in sheet for attendance, I tell the students to place their cell phone numbers beside their names. I then copy the first list and hand a copy to everyone in the class. I do this for two reasons: One, if I am stuck, I can at least call a few people in order to inform them that I am on my way. Two, this allows students access to each other's phone number should they miss an assignment. Each student can call one another to see what he/she might have missed, instead of calling the professor for every missed class. Today,

128

students who miss class will often email the professor. This is still much easier than calling and hoping to get in touch immediately. Also, with Black Board, the teacher can post all the notices regarding scheduling and assignments making things more convenient for the students and staff alike.

In any event, many if not all of these concerns have been addressed by the use of new technology. That was not the case when I started teaching. Southern simply did not have a protocol for informing the class of last minute cancellations. In any event, I believe there should be a back-up protocol to address these issues. I mention this primarily for situations where the professor may be at school while there is a black out. There could very well be situations where the cell phones and the computers are or become inoperable. I witnessed one situation where there was a University wide black-out due to a motor vehicle accident hitting a utility line. Also, I have witnessed the need to cut the power in certain type of emergencies. When those situations arise there really has to be a way to communicate to avoid needless trips to school (when classes have been canceled) for one reason or another. Of course, the time frame often comes into play. If cancellations occur early enough, there is really no issue. It simply becomes much more difficult when the cancellation occurs at the last minute. In that type of situation the students normally arrive and are simply told "class has been canceled". This is so frustrating to students and faculty.

Chapter Nine:
Administrative Issues and Problems for President Joe

Unfortunately, many if not all of the Administrative Issues I notice today have to do with funding. The following observations are key suggestions to resolution of those issues.

CLASSES AT SOUTHERN CONNECTICUT STATE UNIVERSITY

I am seeing that many of the classes being offered are done so very late. If classes are offered late, or fill up early, students often are unable to fulfill their credit requirements in order to graduate on time. This happens to many of the students I know. It also happened to my daughter, Eva Anne. Students, as a result of this, would need to attend an extra semester because they could not get the classes they needed on time. This is simply unacceptable. This has to be remedied since it is indicative of severe financial strain and/or possibly poor criteria for maintaining future accreditation. I simply mean such constant strain jeopardizes Southern's accreditation and reputation. The mission of this School IS NOT TO MAKE MONEY AT THE STUDENTS' EXPENSE. The Administration knows this. The University's failure to graduate its students on time due to these issues jeopardizes the University Mission. Students eligible to graduate on time should be able to do so. Classes needed should not and cannot be constantly out of reach. This alone will cause, besides unnecessary delay, an attrition we cannot justify. Students will then be forced to drop out, or look elsewhere for classes they so desperately need.

The Administration must do more to ensure course offerings allowing our students to complete their four-year degrees on time. This problem should only occur when the student chooses to take time off. The University should not be taking time off from its mission of graduating its students on time.

SUMMER CLASSES

I also saw (first hand) that summer classes are very expensive. I simply do not get it. When I started teaching summer classes were always filled. Today, it is a ghost town at Southern. No one can afford the cost. Why doesn't the school lower the cost to make sure its summer classes are filled? Why do we not see classes on Saturdays and Sundays? This could help with the issue mentioned above to ensure that students simply graduate on time. I do not see why the cost of summer school is so much higher than the standard classes offered during the fall and spring. This too needs review and correction sooner than later.

Further, the School can also offer a pre-admission program for those students who are questionable due to poor board scores. This would allow students to take a summer course at their own expense to help admissions determine whether they can do the course work if their SAT scores are below the required scores. If the student passes, he/ she can then be admitted to the University. This is just a suggestion for thought.

There should be more use of creativity. Why can't we offer retraining courses to Local Police Departments and have our Professors teach these classes. These classes can be offered over the summer or on weekends. Why do we not utilize our great physical plant to accomplish some of the goals needed in our city and state? This also fosters great public relations. It makes our University an integral part of the City and State.

We could reach out to different employers for purposes of offering management courses for supervisors. We could train law enforcement in use of droans for purposes of practical and legal use requirements. We have Professor Vern Williams who would teach the practical aspects. This class is needed and could be filled with state and local police officers and other law enforcement officials. Why isn't this being done to attract attendance here at Southern? I think more can be done in this regard.

TRIMESTERS

One other way to address the issues discussed above may be to admit students three times a year. This would then offer hope to students to not only get the classes they need but will encourage students to graduate before the four years are up. Further, this would allow graduations three times a year. I think it is something that should be considered. In any event, the current system is not working very well and needs to be reviewed. We could also offer trimesters with an eye to getting graduates to take our graduate courses once we accelerate our undergraduate curriculum. This could help to improve our Graduate Studies Program.

NATIONAL SEARCHES AND AN ABUSE OF COMMON SENSE

I love higher education and quite frankly cannot understand some of the thinking regarding potential job searches. Although written from my experience, I do not intend to focus on any one person. I do not aim any of these criticisms at any of our current administrators. These are simply my observations and concerns.

Sometimes when a position becomes vacant, I see that the school will conduct a National Search. I believe that this is done to attempt to get the best possible talent for the position. Unfortunately, the idea of a national search is self-defeating. Let's say, for example, that Southern is in need of a President. We conducted a national search for candidates. It seeks to obtain the best qualified candidates from where ever. This is all well and good.

My problem is that if someone is selected from California, that person may not be aware of the current political climate in Connecticut. When Michael Adante was President he knew people. He could make a call and get through the political thicket. An outsider will not be able to do that very well. I think an outsider would need to meet with (and be briefed by) key Connecticut Politicians before taking the job. Bringing someone in from afar, unaware of the unique political issues and divisiveness in Connecticut simply begs failure. If the selection process is to remain as it is, there must be immediate changes. Presidents hired should be on probation to determine whether he/she can meet the unique challenges this states mandates. This job is more than running a Great University. It includes maintaining the required functions of the job. It also includes obtaining the required funding. It requires sustainability. It does not mean the person should roll over and die. The current hiring process has the seeds to its own destruction. What an incredible waste of time and money. I am sure the Governor realizes this more than anyone else. It is time to wake up. It is time to streamline every cost measure for cost effectiveness. Why isn't everyone accountable? Why does it appear that everyone has an unlimited budget to waste money? This has got to stop.

Perhaps the President should initiate a "cost savings" plan. It could include the old fashioned suggestion box. Students who make a good cost saving suggestion should possibly get a free course. I am sure many of our students and/or staff could make a ton of suggestions to save money. Of course, this is just a thought.

The President must have access to those key political figures that can make things happen. He/she must be pro-active and sail to protect the University Mission. If he/she is in for the ride, then he/she must go. There should be a task force to help aid the President in this regard almost like a cabinet. Unfortunately, the talent is often at the School and simply overlooked. This is a waste of vital resources and services. This type of spending is simply not well justified. Does the State have to go bankrupt before anyone acts. Fiscal Responsibility is "everyone's business". It is not the job of the Legislature alone. It is my obligation and your obligation. How can so many educated people ignore this simple fact. The Mission of all Agencies must be to "act in the Public Interest". This means to provide a quality education at the lowest most efficient price. The way we are heading illustrates a clear "betrayal of the public trust".

The best President that I could see, was Michael Adante. He knew how to achieve the Mission. He put things in order by prioritizing first. He then progressed a step at a time to accomplish those things on his list. There is no trick to it. His record was successful because of his hard work and dedication. Of course, it surely did not hurt to know people and to be from Connecticut. He was a person with a vision. He was able to convince others that his vision was the mission of the school.

LACK OF COOPERATION AMONG STATE AGENCIES

Donald Trump is our President. His various tweets and vacillation on both foreign and domestic policies have worked havoc on our citizens and allies. This is very clear regarding "Immigration Policy". Let me explain.

President Trump has authorized immigration officials to deport aliens. With no prioritizing of deportations, U.S. Officials have sought to deport illegals with families including children who are citizens and clumped these aliens together with convicted aliens. Many aliens have sought Asylum in Churches and Cities like New Haven known as Sanctuary Cities. This poses difficulty for Southern Connecticut Administrators and the President of the University. Southern Connecticut is a State Institution. Our Governor Malloy has already said that he does not support the Trump Administration's Immigration policies. The Governor seems to be in favor of Safety Zones like New Haven and our Connecticut State University System.

This means that if an illegal alien is attending school here as a student at Southern, that he/she should and would be harbored by the State. What happens when Federal Immigration Officials seek to come on campus to detain specific students or to execute a warrant?

The State is working on that answer. First, the Feds would need to be accompanied by the State Police. This means, at the very least, that the President will be placed on notice. Does he know what to do? He would need to call the Office of the Attorney General for help. I wonder if President Joe knows who to call and who to specifically speak with? My concern is that the protocol in essence is vague or no protocol at all. The

State must immediately and forthwith clarify what is to be done. We are looking to the President of the University for guidance and I am sure the guidance is simply not there because it does not exist. He is or will be placed on standby while the AG figures out what to do. That is, if he can get through to someone. Have you ever tried calling?

This is so important. Students admitted here have a constitutional right to proceed with their studies. It is a protected right under the due process clause of the Fourteenth Amendment, including the liberty and property provisions. It is both a substantive and procedural due process right. Further, there are Fifth Amendment rights that may be implicated. Under the Prune Yard cases, many times the State Constitutional guarantees are "judicially interpreted" to be broader than the Federal provisions. We, as professors and administrators have a duty to protect our students. I don't feel like that duty is being taken very seriously as the lack of clear protocol illustrates.

I will clarify. If we were grade school teachers and we happened to see a student come to school with severe bruises, we would have an obligation to report (a duty) and try to help protect that student from any harm or imminent harm. The comparison applies here. The State of Connecticut Constitution prohibits the unlawful segregation of people. Illegal and Legal Aliens, like citizens, are people and make up the student population. With the arbitrary and capricious way the Trump Administration is carrying out its Immigration Policies, I see any aid whatsoever given to this illegal action is tantamount to helping those authorities violate the constitutional rights of all of our students, not just those of illegal alien status. We then fail to provide an environment conducive to learning. We thus violate our own Mission. This is simply as bad as violating the First Amendment rights of our students. No University wants a reputation for violating the constitutional rights of its students. This is serious business.

My plea here is simple. There must be a co-operative effort among State Agencies for clarity. There must be a protocol that protects our students-PERIOD. The dichotomy of legal or illegal makes little sense when these people are our students. The President of our Great University should ask the Attorney General to provide an Attorney General Opinion which immediately clarifies the protocol to protect our students. Any lack of action in this regard is suspect and a neglect of duty. I guess we could wait and see what happens. Of course, by then it would be too late. Action is needed right now.

FUTURE OF HIGHER EDUCATION IN CONNECTICUT

The Connecticut University System has been instrumental in keeping tuition rates down for Connecticut residents. This has always been the case. Our State Universities have always offered a quality education at bargain-rate tuition. Things are changing today which make our Connecticut University System less competitive. Unless these challenges are adequately addressed, we will lose our edge and forfeit our ratings.

First, Massachusetts and New York are offering tuition free college to students in those states. I realize there is a short residency requirement, but this new issue may soon cause Connecticut State Universities to lose students. Why would a student in Connecticut pay tuition in Connecticut if he or she could go to Massachusetts or New York for free? There are many factors that go into that consideration. If a student is working in Connecticut and gets tuition reimbursement in some form, that may simply be good enough to stay. If a student has a job and family here in Connecticut and if his/her spouse also works in Connecticut, that may be another consideration favoring his/her decision to stay in Connecticut.

The problem is that most of the Connecticut Graduates from our colleges and universities are simply moving out of state because of the poor economic climate in Connecticut. As long as this is the case, the Connecticut University System will have real and substantial challenges.

What can be done? I suppose we could consolidate, as is the current plan. It seems a little unfair that UConn, my Alma Mater, seems to be expanding while all the other state colleges and universities are barely surviving. The Administrators must research and devise a plan based upon actual population and yearly trends. Further, there needs to be an agreement or commitment from the General Assembly and the Governor that funds set-aside for higher education must not be touched. Today, with the current state of budget cuts, and union give-backs, there is and can be no plan to ensure higher educational commitment and success in this state. UConn does not seem to have this problem. The Flagship University has all the perks. This trend is suicide for the smaller state colleges and universities. A task force should be devised to review these issues with a firm date to report back to state officials.

We could also offer classes in conjunction with agreements with the towns for local police officers, for example. By entering into pacts with different local agencies, we can maintain a steady stream of students which could keep our enrollment up.

We could also offer courses of public interest. At Southern, we have a Sociology Professor who is skilled in Droan Law. His courses could attract many different groups and possibly encourage a new type of agreement with law enforcement and/or security companies regarding the use of Droans in society. How to license, regulate, etc.

Brainstorming is the best way to compete. Also, we could offer joint programs with other major universities both in the United States and Abroad might help. Southern has also many interdepartmental courses which use joint efforts of various departments to teach certain classes. This could give us an edge in some respects if these classes are creatively offered and pursued.

Unless and until the Connecticut General Assembly comes together and properly considers the commitment it deserves to make to higher education in this state, I see no answer coming. I do see brave men and women who work hard to keep their schools going. I see Administrators and State Employees working hard to overcome obstacles that no one should have to endure. I see layoffs at the bottom and nothing at the top. When the Governor mentions layoffs, he never mentions people making $150,000 or more. He mentions the poor secretaries and maintenance people who make no where near the salaries of higher state wage earners.

Unless something can be done to keep our schools competitive, I do not see an immediate answer. Keeping the tuition low is always a given. Possibly encouraging State and Federal help to our students regarding "Student Forgiveness" programs is another option. Our two state senators have initiated such programs for Congressional approval. Until there are incentives given to students to not only go to school in

Connecticut, but to remain and work here in Connecticut, I unfortunately see mass migrations to other states. This will lower our number of residents in the state and will shrink our already dwindling tax base. We see this downward spiral which is clearly affecting our state legislature's attempt to balance an already shrinking budget. Money is key to correcting many of these issues. How do we expect our teachers' to properly address these issues? Clearly the answer is not to give up their pensions. It really has a lot to do with fiscal responsibility. Is it fair, though, to put the brunt of all this on the University Professors? I simply cannot comprehend the thought process making the state employees responsible every time the state is in trouble. The answers here are a bit more complex than this. Part of the blame falls on the Governor and part of the blame falls on the General Assembly. Keep in mind that once the Indian Casino's opened in Connecticut, the state of Connecticut entered into a contract (treaty) with the Tribes to pay a portion of their slot revenue to the state. Had those funds from 1987 on been saved, Connecticut would have been free and clear of the great recession and would have been free of all its current fiscal problems. Ask the state reps about this and their reply will be: "The State is not good at saving money". Well, my response is "Why not"? The state at this point had just implemented the state income tax. The money was coming in like you would not believe. Where, by God, has it all gone? It was clearly mismanaged. It is all gone.

Today, we suffer. All state employees are suffering through this. Those still working in higher education are concerned about the future. Will the college or university still be around? We surely hope so. I just hate to see the burden of these issues being placed upon the hard-working professors and staff working day to day to keep these operations going. It just does not seem fair. It is also unfair to our hard-working students. It is very difficult for students attending college to think about the possible closure of their institution. What would their diplomas be worth then?

The issues discussed are real and divisive. No one wants to see college closures. No one wants to see mass-migrations. No one wants to see fiscal mismanagement. These points are clear. Fiscal management must be the sole criteria in order to ensure the success of the Connecticut State University System. Connecticut has a tough road ahead. The answers are hard to obtain. The struggle must address each crisis in an orderly and prioritized way. Nobody ever said being a Political Science Professor is easy. One great Political Scientist did say that educating the world of the problem is simply not enough.

CONCLUSION

One realizes that learning has no direct path to riches. Often, the most intelligent and creative people are those who have a goal or mission and who simply fulfill that goal by hard work and sweat. Our society often equates success with wealth. Perhaps modern society has fostered this myth regarding success.

One thing, however, is for certain. Students who come to our University, must be assured that they will learn and graduate with a quality education at a reasonable price. The mission of our Public Universities must be embraced and fulfilled. The quality of our education cannot suffer due to political constraints.

Our teachers, our administrators, our legislators, and our public must learn to prioritize our values to make sure our Institutions of Higher Education are not jeopardized or taken for granted. The current political atmosphere is toxic to our mission. This is true at both the Federal and the State levels. This toxicity challenges the very foundation of our learning institutions. I see this in Connecticut because of the uncertain budgetary conditions of our state. Our Educational System is ill-equipped for generating revenue. It is unfair, illogical, and simply inconsistent with the Mission of our Great Public Universities to require this to occur. We are not money makers.

Success often brings the desired results. Our success must be measured by the quality of our Educational Institutions. Like Public Safety, some policies cannot be measured by cost. Some things, like Education, must be given top priority at all costs.

These are a few of my thoughts. We often view our environment by the glasses we are accustomed to wear. My views of higher education may be different from your views. Although we always try to remain objective, it is hard when we are the subject of the conversation.

As I think back, I consider my observations to be the product of my many years at Southern. These observations I share are my observations. They are fair observations. They are clear as far as I can recollect. Unfortunately, they are biased in favor of law and equity. They are tarnished by my legal views.

Make no mistake about it, though, my teaching experience has had a profound effect on me. I hope that the experiences shared have also been as beneficial to others.

T
H
E

E
N
D
!

"Epilogue"

In closing, a few comments are needed. As I was finishing this book, some of my observations about the Trump Administration are also made by James Comey's recent book, "A Higher Loyalty". Although I plan to read this book, I at no time used or taken any of Mr. Comey's ideas. My observations are mine and made only from my recollection of events pertaining to the Trump Administration. I do certify that I at no time copied, stole, or used Mr. Comey's thoughts and/or impressions.

My writing was simply my way of telling my memory of events at Southern. I humbly apologize, once again, for any errors of fact that I might have made. Much of my writing focuses on my upbringing. Please understand that my writing was never meant to hurt or harm anyone. My intent was to share my wonderful memories of a great school. I simply wanted to share my thoughts and memories of my colleagues and their contributions.

Last, I felt it necessary to share these memories. I refer to them as golden.

Frank P. Cannatelli

ABOUT THE AUTHOR

Frank was born on Sept. 16th, 1954 in Meriden, Connecticut. He attended parochial school before attending Platt High School also in Meriden. He attended the University of Connecticut where Frank received a Bachelors with "honors" in Political Science. Frank then went on to law school graduating in 1987. (California Western and UB Law with Summer Classes in Evidence and Article Nine at UConn Law School).

Frank began teaching at Southern in 1986. He continued to teach up through his retirement in 2017. Frank continues to teach classes in United States Government, United States Legal Systems, Administrative Law and Public Policy, Constitutional Law, and United States Political Issues. He also has experience teaching Sophomore English at the high school level.

Now that Frank is retired, he enjoys involvement with state retiree issues and teaches SAT preparatory classes to high school students. He also practices law on a part time basis in his firm, Cannatelli Law, LLC. Frank can always be reached at his email address: Cannatellilaw@aol.com. He states that all emails will be acknowledged. Frank further certifies that he purposely has selected the cheapest publication of this book in anticipation of a wide distribution. He hopes he is not presumptuous in making that statement.

Last, the author certifies that $5.00 of every sale of this book will be donated to Saint Jude Children's Research Hospital, 262 Danny Thomas Place, Memphis, Tn. 38105 (1-800-822-6344).

REFERENCES

1. Dale Carnegie, "How to Win Friends and Influence People", (Simon & Schuster), Oct. 1936: ISBN: 1-4391-6734-6. (Mentioned on page 22 but not quoted).

2. Stephen Hawking, "A Brief History of Time", (NY Bantum Books), 1988: ISBN: 978-0-553-10953-5. (Mentioned on page 51 but not quoted).

3. Samuel Lubell, "The Future of American Politics", (Greenwood-Heinemann Publishing), 1952: ISBN: 0313243778. (Mentioned on page 57 and 60 but not quoted).

4. Chinua Achebe, "Things Fall Apart", (William Heinemann Ltd.), 1958: ISBN: 9780385474542. (Mentioned on pages 57-61 but not quoted).

5. Alexander Bickel, "The Least Dangerous Branch", (Bobbs-Merrill Company Inc.), 1962: ISBN: -13: 978-0300032994. (Mentioned on pages 64-65 but not quoted).

6. Henry Kissinger, "A World Restored", (Boston: Houghton Mifflin), 1957: ISBN: 978055017573. (Mentioned on pages 67-68 but not quoted).

7. James Barber, "The Presidential Character: Predicting Performance in the White House", 1972 (but updated in 1977, 1985 and 1992): ISBN-13:978-020565259X. (Mentioned on pages 90-94 but not quoted). (Barber's theme is summarized in an article by John Dean, "Active/Negative Trump is doomed to follow Nixon". See, http://www.newsweek.com/activenegative-trump-doomed-follow-nixon-616641.

8. James Comey, "A Higher Loyalty", 2018 (April 17th): ISBN 9781250192462. Mentioned on page 144. (Mentioned but not quoted).